The Education Act, 1918

The Education Act, 1918

Lawrence Andrews
Christ Church College, Canterbury, Kent
University of London

Routledge & Kegan Paul
London, Henley and Boston

First published in 1976
by Routledge & Kegan Paul Ltd
39 Store Street,
London WC1E 7DD,
Broadway House,
Newtown Road,
Henley-on-Thames,
Oxon RG9 1EN and
9 Park Street,
Boston, Mass. 02108, USA
Manuscript typed by Vera Taggart
Printed and bound in Great Britain by
Morrison & Gibb Ltd, London and Edinburgh

ISBN 0 7100 8409 9

The Students Library of Education has been designed to meet the needs of students of Education at Colleges of Education and at University Institutes and Departments. It will also be valuable for practising teachers and educationists. The series takes full account of the latest developments in teacher-training and of new methods and approaches in education. Separate volumes will provide authoritative and up-to-date accounts of the topics within the major fields of sociology, philosophy and history of education, educational psychology, and method. Care has been taken that specialist topics are treated lucidly and usefully for the non-specialist reader. Altogether, the Students Library of Education will provide a comprehensive introduction and guide to anyone concerned with the study of education, and with educational theory and practice.

Contents

Contents

The Education Act, 1918

Preface

This case-study of the Education Act, 1918, is an attempt
to evaluate the importance of the Act in the development
of educational history in England and Wales. To do this,
the situation which faced H.A.L. Fisher when he became
President of the Board of Education in December 1916 with
the formation of Lloyd George's first coalition government
is outlined. Then the important stages in the formation
of the 1917 Education Bill and the forces aligned against
it are related, together with an account of its withdrawal. The 1918 Education Bill is then analysed and the
reaction of pressure groups both inside and outside
Parliament to it are depicted. In chapter 4, the impact
of the post-war years and the educational development in
these years are discussed. The work ends with the fall
of Lloyd George's Coalition government in October 1922.

Throughout the book, the Education Bills and then the
Act are placed against the social, political and economic
movements of the times. The First World War forms a
sombre background.

To write the book, War Cabinet and Cabinet papers have
been studied as well as the reports and documents of the
Board of Education. This knowledge has been supplemented
by an analysis of the private papers of the many pressure
groups interested in the 1917 and 1918 Education Bills.

A study of Fisher's personal papers at the Bodleian
Library, Oxford, have proved helpful as well as a consideration of his publications and conversations with people
who knew him.

In the preparation of the manuscript, my wife has provided invaluable assistance. The Editor's guidance has
also been much appreciated, although the final work
remains the responsibility of the author.

Abbreviations

For reference to sources listed in the Bibliography, the following abbreviations are used in the text:

WCP   War Cabinet Papers, Public Record Office, London
CP   Cabinet Papers, Public Record Office, London
BEP   Board of Education Papers, Public Record Office, London
RBE   Report of the Board of Education, HMSO
PP   Private Papers
MEP   Ministry of Education Papers
ME   Ministry of Education
TES   The Times Educational Supplement
CCA   County Councils Association
CBI   Confederation of British Industries
NUT   National Union of Teachers
WEA   Workers' Education Association

Chapter one

The prologue

CAUSES FOR CONCERN

During the changing, complex, sometimes turbulent but
formative period that elapsed between the accession of
King Edward VII as British sovereign on 22 January 1901,
following the death of his mother, Queen Victoria, and
the outbreak of the First World War on 4 August 1914,
perceptive observers in Britain became increasingly
concerned at the challenge to Britain's supremacy in the
world by the USA, Germany and Japan. Britain still
possessed, however, the largest merchant fleet in the
world, and the strongest navy, and she ruled over and
traded within a vast British Empire.

In addition to being disturbed by the ominous advance-
ment in many directions of other nations, successive
governments in the United Kingdom before the First World
War had to cope with intense political unrest. The calm
of the British Empire, for instance, was disturbed by
disagreement in Ireland.

Demands by women that they should be given the vote
also increased during this period. Up to this time women
had been classed with infants, criminals and lunatics as
unfit to receive the vote although they might own property
and be taxpayers and behave in many respects like Shavian
women.

But of even more concern to governments were the
strikes that took place, such as the dock and railway
strikes of 1911 and the miners' and Port of London
strikes of 1912 (Thomson, 1965, 32). During the early
years of the twentieth century the members of the lower
socio-economic groups increasingly joined the unions,
whose position had been considerably strengthened by the
passing of the Trade Disputes Act of 1906, in order to
express their impatience at the slow progress towards

social reform. In their agitation, they were joined by
the expanding and articulate suburban white-collar lower
middle class (depicted, for example, in the novels of
H.G. Wells and Arnold Bennett), who helped to run the
Civil Service, the banks, the large industries, and to
man the firms dealing with insurance, accountancy and
commerce.

PRESSURES FOR EDUCATIONAL REFORM

Inextricably interwoven into the demands of the lower
socio-economic groups for more social reform were requests
for more equality of opportunity in education as the
value of acquiring a sound education was appreciated ever
more keenly. Included in these demands were more
opportunities for boys and girls to obtain a secondary
education in the exclusive but expanding, fee-paying,
county secondary grammar schools founded and maintained
by councils following the passing of the 1902 Balfour
Education Act. Higher academic work and more variety of
curriculum in the many thousands of all-age elementary
schools which the majority of the school population
attended from the ages of 5 to about 13 or 14 were other
requests. The Cockerton judgment of 1900 had limited this
(Barnard, 1961, 208-9).

These elementary schools, furthermore, were either
provided schools, which meant, under the terms of the 1902
Education Act, that they came under the jurisdiction of
the local education authority and in which religious
instruction unconnected with the formulary and beliefs of
any particular denomination was taught, or non-provided,
which meant that they were maintained by the churches.
These included the Church of England, Roman Catholic and
Nonconformist churches. In the non-provided, or voluntary, schools, religious education of the particular
Church was given. This arrangement of provided and confessional schools was known as the Dual System.

A highly competitive, free-place system was introduced
in 1907 under Article 20 of the Regulations for Secondary
Schools to enable children at the age of 11 to transfer
from the elementary school to the grammar school but the
numbers who did so were small and did not satisfy demands
for more children to receive a secondary education.

There were, during the period before the First World
War, movements in state education which attempted to
meet the accusations that educational provision did not
meet the requirements of the age. Thus Robert Morant's
'Elementary School Code' of 1904 pointed the way to a more

enlightened approach to elementary school teaching. He
was Permanent Secretary to the Board of Education at this
time and had taken an active part in the passing of the
1902 Education Act. His regulations for secondary schools
of the same year are considered less successful because
it is estimated that they were influenced too much by the
curricula and approach to teaching of the endowed grammar
schools and independent public schools. To meet the
requests for schools with a vocational bias which would
enable boys and girls to enter industry and commerce at
about the age of 16, central schools appeared from 1911,
as did, from 1913, schools variously known as junior
technical schools, technical high schools or trade
schools (Lawson and Silver, 1973, 376). More attention
was directed, besides, to the teaching of science in
schools in order to produce more scientists for the
country.

A movement in education before the First World War
which influenced state education, moreover, was composed
of schools now often referred to as progressive schools,
such as Bedales, Abbotsholme and Homer Lane's 'Little
Commonwealth'. This movement sought ways of developing a
new freedom for children (Stewart, 1972, part three).

The public schools, as well, with their emphasis on the
house system, prefect system, team games and the public
school spirit, still considerably influenced secondary
education. As ideas of social equality, however, unfolded
during the.twentieth century, criticism increased of the
public schools for providing an education for a privileged
minority. As, too, the state system of education grew
after the passing of the 1902 Education Act it was not
only felt that the Board of Education should have some
knowledge of the number of schools in the independent sector of education but that it should be able to ensure that
the education in the private sector did not fall markedly
below that of the maintained schools of the local
education authorities.

COLLECTIVISM

To meet the demands for social reform and to ensure that
Britain was not falling behind other countries in so many
aspects, the foremost reaction of successive Liberal
governments, with large majorities in the House of
Commons following the landslide victory in the 1906
General Election, was to hasten the movement towards
collectivism. By this was meant more intervention by the
state in the lives of the population. The principles of

laissez-faire, such as free trade, free currency and free
enterprise were still accepted by many politicians,
industrialists and civil servants but it was increasingly
accepted that a measure of collectivism was necessary in
order to safeguard certain vital interests of the nation.
Thus, for example, when Herbert Henry Asquith, the Liberal
MP for East Fife, became Prime Minister in April 1908, the
Old Age Pensions Act was passed in the same year. Soon
after, in 1911, the National Health Insurance Act of
Lloyd George, the Liberal and Welsh Nationalist MP for
Carnavon, and Chancellor of the Exchequer, attempted to
solve the problem of ill-health and unemployment.

   But it was now also accepted that it was not only
necessary to protect and improve the lives of men and
women of all ages but that the health of the children in
all its aspects had to be improved, developed and
protected as well. It was pointed out, too, that it was
of limited use building new elementary schools, and
improving teaching, when many of the children who attended
were unable to benefit because of their inadequate
physical health. Since the Second Boer War (1899-1902),
when recruitment for the British forces had revealed the
low physical standard of many of the men examined, the
nation had become increasingly concerned at the problem of
physical deterioration.

   In order to combat malnutrition and ill-health the
government provided school meals (but not yet school milk)
and introduced medical inspection although not providing
treatment. Under the Education (Provision of Meals) Act,
1906, local education authorities were empowered to form
school canteen committees which were to provide, by
levying a rate not exceeding a ½d in the £, suitable meals
at a cheap rate for those children who were unable by
reason of lack of food to take full advantage of the
education provided (Andrews, 1972, 70-5).

   The state system of school medical inspection began in
this country as a result of the Education (Administrative
Provisions) Act, 1907, which imposed on all local
education authorities the duty of providing for the
medical inspection of children, immediately before, or at
the time of, or as soon as possible after, admission to
school, and on such other occasions as the Board of
Education might direct.

   Authorities were also empowered to establish vacation
schools and classes, play centres, or other means of
recreation during the holidays, or at other times, either
in the school itself, or elsewhere, for example, in the
country. By 1915, all local education authorities had
appointed a school medical staff, although these staffs

were to be depleted during the First World War (ME, 1950, VI).

The 1912 Report of the Departmental Committee appointed to inquire into 'Certain Questions in Connection with the Playgrounds of Public Elementary Schools' was, however, a sober document revealing not only the very limited amount of playing space available in the elementary schools but also what local authorities and teachers had done, and were doing, on their own initiative, to organise games for children. Co-operation between education and parks committees was therefore encouraged. By the time of the First World War, Birmingham and Manchester, for example, were being quoted by the Board of Education in the Report of the Chief Medical Officer for 1915 as places where there had been successful co-operation between education and parks committees to provide recreational facilities for young people.

The needs of the mentally handicapped were also considered during this period and a Mental Deficiency Act was passed in 1913. In 1908, a Children's Charter set up special Children's Courts for children who had committed crimes. In 1914, under the Education (Provision of Meals) Act, the limit of a ½d rate stipulated by the 1906 Act was removed. The grant providing for school meals was also increased.

The collectivist movement was not viewed favourably by all. Some feared it, seeing it as a symbol of the encroaching, absolute, sovereign power of the 'leviathan' of the welfare state. Thus A.V. Dicey, the eminent jurist, did not support the 1906 Education (Provision of Meals) Act, under which school meals could be provided for necessitous children, because he believed that parents were being deprived of their responsibility for the care of their children by intervention of the central government. In his 'Law and Public Opinion in England' (1914, passim), Dicey did not deny that a starving boy might find it difficult to learn the rules of arithmetic but it did not necessarily follow for him that a local authority should provide every hungry child at school with a meal. Because of this, Dicey submitted that parents should be disenfranchised if they could not pay for the meals of their children. He therefore placed the 1906 Meals Act in the same category as the Old Age Pensions Act, 1908, the National Insurance Act, 1911, the Trade Disputes Act, 1906, the Trade Union Act, 1913, the Acts fixing a minimum rate of wages, the Mental Deficiency Act, 1913, the Coal Mines Regulation Act, 1908, and the Finance (1909-10) Act, 1910, as evidence of the adverse progress of statism in the years preceding the First World War.

Supporters of Dicey's point of view, moreover, maintained that the welfare work that was needed in the nation could be carried out by voluntary bodies such as the Charity Organisation Society, and the application of the Poor Law, as it had been done up until then.

THE EMPLOYMENT OF CHILDREN AND RAISING THE SCHOOL-LEAVING AGE

A major obstacle to the creation of an education system in this country and an impediment in the development of a fit nation had been the employment of children outside school hours. But through the Employment of Children Act, 1903, an attempt had been made to regulate some of the anomalies in the employment of children. The Education (Administrative Provisions) Act, 1907, and the Education (Scotland) Act, 1908, also provided the local authorities in Great Britain with officers who could carry out the provisions of the 1903 Employment Act. The 1910 Choice of Employment Act, moreover, had built upon the foundations laid by the 1903 Act, and had enabled local authorities to make arrangements, subject to the approval of the Board of Education, to give assistance to boys and girls under 17 in their choice of suitable employment. It was hoped in this way to protect more the educational interests of children who left the elementary schools and to lessen the number of those who entered 'blind alley' employment. By the time of the First World War, there were still, however, approximately 300,000 children in England and Wales aged under 14 employed in factories, mines and agriculture and in miscellaneous street trading occupations, such as newspaper, ice cream, flower and match selling, organ grinding and railway touting (Keeling, 1914, passim).

Another hindrance to the creation of a satisfactory education system in this country and a check on national progress had been the adverse effects of the half-time system of employment on both children and schools. During the early years of the twentieth century, therefore, there was increasing pressure for this system to be abolished. One voluntary lobby which formed to do this was the Half-Time Council with its headquarters at Rochdale in Lancashire.

By the time of the First World War, the age at which exemption from attending school might still be obtained was 12, although some by-laws of local education authorities allowed this at 11 and 13. Under what was considered the proper half-time system of employment the child

attended, say, the mill for half a day and the school for
the other half, with the times spent in these places being
reversed the following week. There were, however, variations of this arrangement. The half-time system, moreover, was mainly to be found in Lancashire, where children
were chiefly employed in the cotton mills, in Yorkshire,
where the staple industry was worsted spinning and
weaving, in Cheshire and in agricultural districts. By
1914-15, the Board of Education estimated that there were
69,555 half-timers in England and Wales, although difficulty was found in being accurate about these figures
(RBE, 1917-18, 13).

But linked to the concern which was expressed about the
unfavourable influence of the half-time system of employment on school children, was that about the low and
irregular school-leaving age of many of them, when large
numbers left at 13 and some earlier. Because of this,
there was an increasing desire to raise to 14 the school-
leaving age for all children.

CONCERN FOR THE VERY YOUNG CHILDREN AND THE YOUTHFUL
SCHOOL-LEAVER

As part of the policy of improving the standard of
education in the country, enquiries were also carried out
during the years before the First World War into the sort
of guidance which was provided for very young children,
for those who were about to leave school, and for the
young wage-earner. Thus, in 1905, women inspectors of
the Board of Education reported on children under 5
attending elementary schools and in 1908 a Consultative
Committee on the school attendance of children below the
age of 5. The over-view expressed was that the physical
and mental development of very young children was being
impeded by the education that they were receiving. In
1911, furthermore, the McMillan sisters pointed the way to
a more progressive interpretation of nursery education
with the foundation of their open-air nursery school at
Deptford, London.

The problems facing the young school-leaver and the
young employee, which had increasingly occupied the
attention of the countries in Western Europe and of the
USA as the twentieth century progressed, the consequences
to the community of neglecting the embryo citizen and
worker during what had come to be called 'the critical
years of adolescence', were analysed by the 1909 Report of
the Consultative Committee on Attendance, Compulsory or
Otherwise, at Continuation Schools. One recommendation of

the Committee was that further education should be available for all those young people up to the age of 17 who
needed it but it was left to the local education authorities of counties and county boroughs to provide suitable
day continuation classes. Attendance at continuation
schools was therefore left as a matter of local option
rather than being made universally compulsory.

An attempt, however, to abolish half-time attendance
at school, to provide for the local education authority
raising the school-leaving age to 14 or 15, or alterna-
tively, or concurrently, requiring attendance at
continuation classes after leaving school for not more
than 150 hours a year up to an age not higher than 16,
was made in Walter Runciman's Bill of early 1911 (PP,
Liberal Party, 1913). Under this Bill it would have been
left open to the authority to arrange compulsory continuation classes either during or after working hours with no
limitation being imposed upon the hours of employment of
a child who commenced attending continuation classes.
The Bill was thus an indication that Liberal thinking was
moving towards the conception of day continuation education.   Unfortunately, it was withdrawn without discussion
because of pressure of time and was not revived because
burning questions of the day such as unemployment and
health insurance, which have been referred to, were given
priority.

LOCAL GOVERNMENT

The difference of opinion as to whether there should be
more state intervention or less was inevitably reflected
in disputes as to how local affairs should be managed.
Schools of thought swayed by the movement towards
collectivism had argued that there should be more
centralization but others had leaned more towards some
form of devolution. Arguing that in industry and commerce
there had been a linking together of forces which had led
to increased efficiency and economy, the former maintained
that such local services as water, transport and police
had best served the community when they had been organized
over large areas and under one control. The supporters of
devolution had stressed that with the increasing demands
of administration, and the growing complexities of modern
life there was a need for a delegation of responsibility.
They were also deeply suspicious of any movement which
might interfere with a thriving local public spirit and
cherished traditions of self-government. Thus, the
borough was feared which might extend the area under its

control at the expense of other authorities because it
was considered that this would be a difficult movement to
stop. It was doubted, as well, if more centralization
was the best plan for all services.

The Consultative Committee of the Board of Education,
which reported in 1908 into the extent and desirability of
devolution of powers by county councils to local district
committees, was unable to make positive recommendations
and confirmed the situation as it already existed. It
also laid stress upon the widely differing circumstances
of the various counties and considered that it would be
difficult, if not impossible, to devise any uniform system
which would give general satisfaction throughout the
country. Social and industrial conditions, as well as the
fact that the people, the educational history and traditions of a county had often nearly as close a bearing
upon its educational organization as its geographical or
industrial conditions, were the main reasons given for
this standpoint.

The pressure for more control from the central authority was viewed favourably in the educational world by some
when it was pointed out that the chief difficulty in
developing a national system of education had been the
fact - stemming from the provisions of the 1902 Education
Act - that among the 317 local education authorities there
were over 120 county councils and county borough councils
responsible for higher education in their areas (which
included secondary education) under Part II of the
Education Act, 1902, and also for elementary education in
their areas under Part III of the 1902 Act. In addition,
over 180 non-county borough councils with a population in
excess of 10,000, and urban district councils with a
population exceeding 20,000, in each case calculated
according to the census of 1901, retained powers for
elementary education under Part III of the Act of 1902.
As there was no obligation on the authorities to co-
operate much had depended on goodwill and understanding.
Many had co-operated, and progress had been made, but, for
a growing number of critics, the system was not a sound
one.

FINANCE

The financial burden of the welfare services and the
growing cost of education, made the Liberal Government
decide to take a sharp look at the system of taxation in
the country. The result was that Sir John Kempe headed,
in 1911, a Departmental Committee to study local taxation.

In its Final Report of March 1914 on Local Taxation,
England and Wales, the Committee recommended the introduction of a system of direct Exchequer grants in aid of
local services, including education, paid as annual Block
Grants in respect of the whole service, but related to
total expenditure, as distinguished from expenditure per
unit, and taking into account the relative wealth or
poverty of areas and their ability to pay.

It was argued that the introduction of a system of
grants based upon expenditure would have the effect of
increasing the control of parliament over the expenditure
of government departments and local authorities on
services aided by grant.

AN EDUCATION BILL

The social and educational reforms to enable Britain to
compete more effectively with other nations in the twentieth century and the new thinking on education in many
areas, meant, however, that pressure mounted from about
1910 for a major Education Act to encapsulate the progressive ideas in education. This meant the supersession of
the 1902 Balfour Act whose provisions were increasingly
considered by many to be incapable of meeting the demands
of the new era.

Subsequently, on 22 July 1913, J.A. Pease (later Lord
Gainford), President of the Board of Education in
Asquith's government, when introducing a one-clause Bill
to give some financial relief to local education authorities, attempted to gather together the movements for
reform in education by outlining the provisions of an
Education Bill which he hoped to present during the autumn
of 1914.

These ideas, however, were shelved when Great Britain
declared war on Germany on 4 August 1914 following the
German invasion of Belgium. In historic words, Edward
Grey, the Foreign Secretary, inspired when watching a
lamplighter in the dusk, summed up the situation by
observing that with the outbreak of the First World War
the lamps went out all over Europe.

Chapter two

The Education Bill, 1917

THE EFFECT OF THE FIRST WORLD WAR

The war that followed, which was the most catastrophic
that the world had seen and lasted for over four years,
brought about profound social changes in Britain.

The status of women in society, for example, was
affected by these changes. As the war progressed and
women released men for combat duties by, for instance,
working on the land and in munition factories, or taking
over all duties in schools, a deeper respect for their
abilities developed. This helped to bring about the
extension of the franchise to some of them under the
Representation of the People Act of 6 February 1918.

The new classes of skilled and semi-skilled labour,
whether in the Forces or in civilian life, which had produced the latest weapons of war used in the battles on
land, sea and air, also augmented the demands for social
and educational reform which had gained momentum before
the First World War but had been muted at its outbreak.

More widespread employment during the war and
increased prosperity in certain areas, meant, also, that
the families benefiting from these developments pressed
for more educational opportunities for their children,
especially for secondary education. This movement linked
up with the demands from the less prosperous members of
the population for reform, generally, in education.

Members of the Forces, such as those convalescing in
'old Blighty', and those either waiting to go to the Front
in Flanders with the boredom, misery, pain, noise and
suffering of the muddy, tunnelled, barbed-wire existence
of trench warfare, or returned from it, were also taking
an increasing interest in problems affecting life and
society. One upshot of this interest was that they were
attending lectures, study groups and classes arranged for

them, sometimes as part of the reconstruction programme.
By 1917, natural science, economics, citizenship and
history were compulsory subjects, too, for all recruits
of 18. All these people helped to make the nation more
receptive to plans for educational reform.

By 1917, also, the nation had become more accustomed to
firmer direction from the central authority in the conduct
of its affairs. The growing movement towards state
collectivism before the war had been accentuated by the
need during wartime for the government to assume tighter
control over the supply and distribution of manpower and
materials, food and other commodities in order that the
war should be waged more successfully.

The small War Cabinets of Asquith, then the Asquithian
Coalition Government of Liberals, Conservatives and Labour
from May 1915, then the Lloyd George Coalition from
December 1916, after Lloyd George became Prime Minister
and First Lord of the Treasury on 7 December 1916, became
the mainspring of policy. In addition, there was a large
number of ministries to supervise the wartime affairs of
the country. Among these was a Department of Scientific
and Industrial Research to harness to the nation's
interests the growth of scientific discovery. Ministries
of Munitions, Food, and Shipping, with other departments,
some linked to the Ministries, kept an economic oversight
on, for example, the supply and distribution of meat and
fats, flour, potatoes, coal, sugar, wheat, oil and seed,
wool and cotton. The railways had automatically passed
into the control of the government at the outbreak of
war. A Canal Control Committee was set up in March 1917
(Taylor, 1965, ch.III).

Social reconstruction had commenced with the founding
of a Ministry of Pensions and the passing of a Pension
Act in 1916, which, with subsequent amendments, embraced
those disabled by the war, widows and children. The
problem of repairing and building new houses was also
receiving government directive. The nation was thus
becoming familiar with the attempts of the central
authority to form a healthier society from the débris of
the old. During 1917, moreover, work was commenced on the
dismantling of the Local Government Board, which included
the Poor Law system, and the building of a Ministry of
Health to help remedy the mental and physical deficiencies
revealed in the population by the war.

Because of these and other pressures - while, it must
be noted, the outcome of the war was still very much
undecided - several lobbies published their proposals for
educational reform. One of these was the Education
Reform Council (Report, 1917) which had been established

on 8 April 1916 at a conference of the Teachers' Guild
Council and was composed of over 100 members, many of
them leading figures of the day in the educational world.
Two others were the Workers' Educational Association
('Highway', passim) founded in 1903 and claiming to be a
federation of 2,150 working class and educational bodies
in England and Wales, and the National Union of Teachers
('TES', December 1916), the largest professional association with a membership of nearly 100,000 out of a teaching
force of about 250,000 teachers in England and Wales.
These suggestions for educational reform between them
covered every aspect of education from that of the very
young child to that of the young school leaver; from the
reform of the organization of the local education
authorities to a streamlining of the examination system
in schools. The proposals received much publicity and
were eagerly discussed by the population, not only because
of their merit but because they were seen as part of a
necessary campaign to improve national life and develop
the Empire. Public opinion had also become more favourable to the thought of increased expenditure on education.

Pressure groups within the political parties had not
been idle, either. In 1913, indicative of the fresh
thinking, J.H. Whitehouse, Liberal MP for Lanarkshire and
author of several books on social and educational reform,
had published 'A National System of Education'. This was
issued with the general approval of the Executive
Committee of the Liberal Education Group in the House of
Commons and advocated wide-ranging reforms. In January
1914 the Unionist Social Reform Committee on Education
had published its Report, 'The Schools and Social
Reform', which F.E. Smith (Unionist, Liverpool, Walton),
then Attorney General, later Lord Birkenhead, in an
introduction, accepted as a basis for Unionist legislation in the future (Hoare, 1914).

At a conference of the Bradford Trades Council in
October 1916, the educational policy of the Labour movement from this time was formulated with, as its main
item, 'universal, free, compulsory secondary education'.
It included, too, raising the school-leaving age to 16,
no exemptions for part-time employment and placing all
schools, colleges and universities under the control of
the state ('TES', 19 October 1916, 180). This meant the
abolition of the Dual system. In 1915, Arthur Henderson
(Lab., Durham, Barnard Castle), one of the Labour leaders,
became President of the Board of Education in Asquith's
Coalition Government.

But another crucial factor that reinforced the pressures for reform was that the demands from agriculture

and industry for child labour had increased during the
war as the men had been called away to fight abroad, with
the result that the numbers of children who claimed
exemption from school attendance on a standard or attendance qualification, or who presented themselves to be
examined for Labour Certificates, rapidly rose.

The disturbing result of the relaxation of the control
of parents, furthermore, with many fathers on military
service and mothers employed in munition-making and
industrial work, was that numerous children suffered from
a want of proper care and discipline. This situation,
with the darkened streets and general war conditions,
threatened to bring about a serious deterioration among
the health and behaviour of the child population.

Consultations and conferences between the Board of
Education, the Director of National Service, the local
education authorities, officers of the Admiralty, Home
Office, Ministry of Labour, Ministry of Munitions,
Ministry of Reconstruction and representatives of voluntary institutions interested in the welfare of the young
were held to consider the provision of educational facilities for young persons who had been abnormally employed
during the war (WCP, GT 1472, 1917; GT 2828, 1917).

At their annual conference at Leicester in May 1918,
it was pointed out to the Superintendents of School
Attendance Departments for England and Wales that the
number of summonses for child neglect in Birmingham, for
example, had increased since the commencement of the war.
In 1917, 4,000 summonses were issued ('Schoolmaster',
1 June 1918, 680).

In 1917, in order to help the children, the Board of
Education encouraged the establishment by local education
authorities and voluntary bodies of play centres for
elementary school children on the lines of the ideas of
Mrs Humphry Ward (Pritchard, 1963, 155-9). These centres
proved of marked value and although there were not many of
them they supplemented the provision of boys' and girls'
clubs, brigades, and similar organizations which were also
increasing as the number of offences committed by young
persons under the age of 16 grew. In order to deal more
systematically with the problem of juvenile delinquency,
a Juvenile Organization Committee, consisting of social
and welfare workers, was established by the Home Office
(RBE, 1917-18, 8-9).

In a variety of ways the schools contributed to the war
effort during the years of combat by supporting, for
instance, the National Savings movement and cultivating
allotments. But the need for economy led to the restriction of expenditure on equipment and premises and to the

cessation of building. Some two hundred school buildings
were also occupied by the Army and Navy, with half of
these being used as hospitals. About 138,000 school children had to be accommodated, because of this, in temporary
premises, chapels, Sunday schools and similar buildings.
In certain areas it was necessary, in order to educate
the children, to use the available buildings on a double
shift system because of the shortage of accommodation
(ibid., 1914-15, 17-18).

From about the summer of 1916, therefore, because of
the growing demand for reform, the word 'reconstruction'
became an increasingly familiar one as the war-time Coalition Governments of Asquith and Lloyd George took action
to meet the requests. Committees were established to
indicate the best ways of dealing with the social and
economic problems which would have to be met when the
country returned from a war to a peace-time footing.
During the process, emphasis was placed on the fact that
reconstruction meant the moulding of a better world from
the social and economic conditions which had come into
being during the war and was not a question of rebuilding
the society that had prevailed before it. Eventually, in
March 1916, a Reconstruction Committee was set up by
Asquith with himself as chairman. Ultimately, in March
1917, Lloyd George formed and assumed responsibility for
a Ministry of Reconstruction. This arrangement continued
until August 1917 when Christopher Addison (L., Shore-
ditch, Hoxton), a former Professor of Anatomy at Sheffield
University College and Minister of Munitions during
December 1916, became Minister of Reconstruction (Johnson,
1968, passim).

When the issue of educational reform was considered at
this time many ways were contemplated of investigating the
contemporary situation in education in order to plan for
the future. These reflections included a Royal Commission, a Select Committee of the House of Commons, investi-
gations by the Board of Education or interdepartmental
committees, a committee of the cabinet or a Prime
Minister's committee. The Consultative Committee of the
Board of Education had been suspended during the war.

In June 1916, however, a sub-committee of the Reconstruction Committee, subsequently referred to as the
Education Reviewing Committee, was formed, with the
Marquis of Crewe as chairman, to review the development of
education. L.A. Selby-Bigge, the Permanent Secretary from
1912, and other officials at the Board of Education,
viewed the establishment of the Review Committee with some
apprehension because they did not wish the Board to
become subordinate to it with a corresponding loss of

power over matters of education. But the Reviewing Committee does not seem ever to have met. On 22 March 1917,
the Education Reviewing Committee was dissolved by the
Reconstruction Committee and an educational panel of the
Reconstruction Committee was set up.

Another outcome of the desire to obtain information
about the current situation in education in order to
reconstruct for the future was the establishment in August
1916 of Committees by the Prime Minister (Asquith) to
enquire into the positions of Natural Science and Modern
Languages in the educational system of Great Britain. A
further result was that in April 1916 Arthur Henderson set
up the Departmental Committee on Juvenile Education in
Relation to Employment after the War under the Chairmanship of Herbert Lewis (L., Flintshire), the Parliamentary
Secretary to the Board of Education. But there was an
uneasy relationship between the different committees
appointed to suggest ways in which the educational system
could be improved. Arthur Henderson, however, had come to
the conclusion that a Royal Commission would not be necessary to reform the system of education. He preferred committees of experts appointed by the Prime Minister in consultation with the Board of Education.

On 16 August 1916, Arthur Henderson resigned his
Presidency. He had been unable to devote as much time as
he would have liked to the work at the Board of Education.
He had been more of a Labour than an Education Minister.
Most of the duty of replying to questions in the House
had devolved on Herbert Lewis ('Education', August 1916,
61; Simon, 1965, 343). The Marquis of Crewe succeeded
Henderson.

THE NEW PRESIDENT - H.A.L. FISHER

Shortly afterwards, in December 1916, David Lloyd George,
who was in the process of forming his war-time Coalition
Government, having succeeded Asquith as Prime Minister and
First Lord of the Treasury on 7 December 1916, asked
H.A.L. Fisher, who was then Vice-Chancellor of Sheffield
University and a well-known historian, to succeed the
Marquis of Crewe as President of the Board of Education.
Realizing the need for educational reform and the impor-
tant part that education would play in the reconstruction
of post-war Britain, Lloyd George wanted a man of Fisher's
calibre to take on this vital office. The moment was a
decisive one in the lives of both men.

Fisher hesitated to accept the appointment partly
because he admired Asquith and did not want to give the

impression, by accepting the post, that he was dissatisfied with Asquith's handling of the war, which he was
far from feeling, and partly because he felt that he had
had no parliamentary experience (Fisher, 1940, 91). But
Lloyd George pointed out that a stage had been reached in
the country's history when more educational reform would
be accepted from an educationist than from a politician.
This observation impressed Fisher considerably. The Prime
Minister and Bonar Law (Unionist, Lancashire, S.W.,
Bootle), Chancellor of the Exchequer and Leader of the
House of Commons, who was with Lloyd George during the
interview at the War Office, also assured Fisher that
there would be enough money for educational reform.

Fisher, after he had accepted the post next day, and
after 'confabulation' with his wife in Sheffield, was to
find that A.J. Balfour (Unionist, City of London), Prime
Minister from July 1902 to December 1905 and the recently
appointed Secretary of State for Foreign Affairs was to
give him every assistance. When Fisher told him of his
acceptance of the Presidency, Balfour however, expressed
misgiving that a man of ability was going to the Board
of Education (Ogg, 1947, 62). But it had been Balfour,
when Prime Minister, who had thrown off his indolence and
had fought for the 1902 Education Act in the House of
Commons.

On 14 December 1916, Fisher was sworn in. In the same
month he became, uncontested, a non-party Member of
Parliament for the Hallam division of Sheffield, formerly
a Conservative seat, when the previous occupant was
elevated to the peerage. Fisher's career in politics had
begun, at 51, when he was to make, successfully, the difficult transition from the academic world to that of high
office in politics. A close friendship, moreover, was to
develop between the well-born, former Oxford history don,
whose father had once been Private Secretary to the Prince
of Wales - later King George V - and the flamboyant,
highly articulate, Welsh Prime Minister. Lloyd George's
unwavering support also enabled every proposition that the
President put before the War Cabinet to be carried.

As soon as Fisher became President of the Board of
Education, he and his officials, who throughout the
demanding months and years to follow were to give unswerv-
ing and skilful support to him, set to work to prepare an
Education Bill. Fisher, moreover, conveyed to Lloyd
George on 23 February 1917 that he wished to accept complete responsibility for all plans for educational reform
put before the War Cabinet. This meant that his personal
influence was to be a marked one. It also meant that the
authority of the Education Reviewing Committee and,

subsequently, the educational panel of the Reconstruction Committee, was to be subordinate to that of the Board of Education.

The civil servants at the Board who assisted Fisher in his plans for educational reform included L.A. Selby-Bigge, the Permanent Secretary, who had been a schoolboy with Fisher at Winchester, and who had succeeded Sir Robert Morant (also a Wykehamist and near contemporary) at the Board; W.N. Bruce, Head of the Secondary School Department; J.W. Mackail and E.K. Chambers, who achieved literary distinction, and George Newman, the health specialist.

To help in preparing an Education Bill the inspectors of the Board furnished the President with reports of experiments in education which were being carried out in elementary schools throughout the country. The opinions of people from different walks of life and representing varied interests in education, were also sounded. Two people whose views were familiar to Fisher were Sir Robert Blair, Education Officer of the London County Council, and Lord Haldane, Secretary of State for War 1905-12 and Lord Chancellor 1912-15 (Fisher, 1940, 94-5).

In addition, as part of his duties, Fisher visited schools and other educational establishments in London with the object of making personal contact with teachers and of acquainting himself with examples of each kind of school and institution in the area (WCP, GT 128, 1917).

He was also influenced in his deliberations by his personal experiences as a tutor at New College, Oxford, and as Vice-Chancellor of Sheffield University, which had made him realize how necessary it was to provide opportunities for those young people who lacked them. He regretted, too, that the majority of children did not receive any statutory education after the age of 12, that their health was impaired by the half-time system of schooling and that they worked for long hours outside school hours.

It must be remembered that Fisher was a life-long Liberal who, as a young man, during the early years of the twentieth century, had met surviving exponents of Gladstonian Liberalism with its emphasis on liberty, democratic government, the rights of private property and popular education and had found himself in sympathy with their views. In the great country houses of the times he had not only met and discussed politics and social reform with John Morley, Bryce, Haldane and Lord Rosebery but had also met the young Lloyd George and Winston Churchill (Ogg, 1947, 45). At Oxford, in the 1880s, as an undergraduate, Fisher had been deeply influenced by the

'Prolegomena to Ethics' of T.H. Green who, in turn, had
been inspired by Hegel (Fisher, 1940, 50).

Not a socialist in the sense that he supported the
public ownership of all wealth and property, although he
was sympathetic to more government control, Fisher was
motivated by a deep concern for his fellow man, especially
young people. He was also disturbed by the fact that such
a beautiful country as England was defaced by ugly buildings and smoking factories (Fisher, 1923b, 513).

EDUCATIONAL REFORM

On Tuesday, 20 February 1917, Fisher submitted to the War
Cabinet some of his early proposals for educational reform
contained in Memoranda 'Proposals for Immediate Action',
dated 2 February 1917 and 'General Principles' dated
5 February 1917 (WCP, WC 75, 1917).

In his Memorandum of 5 February 1917 he submitted a
rough estimate of the cost of certain items of the reforms
he was contemplating, pointing out that the figures were
necessarily provisional, the items not exhaustive, and
that it was unwise to entertain the idea that the development of education could be accomplished without the spending of large sums of money by the state.

The figures were (WCP-O, GT 757, 1917):

	£
Cost of raising the school age and abolishing half-time	about 500,000
Cost of establishing nursery schools	rising to 500,000
Cost of compulsory continuation schools on a 50 per cent basis	3,000,000 rising to 4,000,000
Increased grants to secondary schools and a reformed system of examinations	500,000
Establishment of a pension system for secondary and technical teachers	about 130,000
Training of teachers	about 100,000
Scholarships and bursaries	100,000 rising to 300,000

Increased grants for technical education	£
	100,000
	rising to 200,000

At this meeting with the War Cabinet, the President drew attention to the needs of the teaching profession stating that elementary teachers were miserably paid and that a discontented teaching class was a social danger. It was not his intention, he also observed, during the war to abolish half-time attendance at schools, nor to raise the school-leaving age. It was considered desirable, however, to obtain statutory recognition of the principle of continued education although he accepted that it might take fifteen years to give full effect to the principle. This observation is interesting in view of what did happen.

The War Cabinet quickly approved of these proposals, as well as Fisher's financial recommendation for a system of percentage grants for education outlined in a Memorandum of 2 February 1917, 'Educational Development', thus overruling objections raised by the Treasury. The President was authorized to proceed with his legislation. This included considerations of increased grants for universities as well as attention being directed to the recommendations of the 1913 Royal Commission on London University. It was agreed, too, that Fisher should consult some of the leading businessmen in the country about the initiation of the system of compulsory day continuation classes for young persons when they had left school. With the carrying of his proposal for a system of percentage grants, Fisher considered that the most important part of the battle had been won (Fisher, 1940, 104).

Later, the pension scheme approved by the Cabinet was extended to include elementary school teachers as well as secondary and technical teachers because the War Cabinet was not only impressed with the importance of raising the quality of the teaching profession and removing from it all reasonable cause of discontent but also considered that at that time 'revolutionary movements were to no small extent fomented by dissatisfied teachers' (WCP-O, GT 1601, 1917).

By March 1917, Fisher was reporting that his Department had been engaged in the development of the educational proposals which had been sanctioned by the War Cabinet. It had also prepared a draft Bill embodying a comprehensive scheme of educational development which had been referred to the Parliamentary draughtsmen.

Regulations providing for a Supplementary Grant to local education authorities for elementary education had also been submitted to the Treasury in order to give

effect to the financial proposals sanctioned by the War
Cabinet.   Later, by a Minute dated 18 April 1917,
Regulations for the payment to local education authorities
of a Supplementary Grant for Elementary Education based on
the recommendations of the Kempe Committee was issued by
the Board of Education.   In paying the grant, the Board,
it was declared in the Regulation, would take into consideration the provision made in each area as a whole for
certain matters helpful to the 'establishment of a complete and satisfactory system of elementary education'.
The payment of adequate salaries to teachers was encouraged in the Regulations.

On 19 April 1917, Fisher submitted to Parliament the
ordinary estimates of the Board of Education for 1917-18
amounting to £15,159,780, with a Supplementary Estimate of
£3,856,000 to local education authorities for elementary
and secondary education and higher salaries for teachers.
He took the opportunity, too, of outlining certain, wide-
ranging reforms in education which he was contemplating.
These plans not only built upon the proposals approved by
the War Cabinet, but also took into account the recommendations of the Lewis Committee in its Report, 'Juvenile
Education in Relation to Employment after the War' of 16
March 1917.   These included the raising of the school-
leaving age to 14 and the provision of compulsory day
continuation schools for young persons aged 14 to 18 for
not less than eight hours a week for forty weeks a year.

Later, in May 1917, while in agreement with the ideals
expressed in the Lewis Report, the Reconstruction Committee argued that 'much stronger action' was required than
the Report suggested.   A comprehensive programme should
have been put forward to be implemented gradually during
the next ten years.   This should have included the raising of the school-leaving age to 16 and the establishment
of compulsory half-time secondary schools up to the age
of 18 (WCP-O, GT 1305, 1917).

On 8 May 1917, Fisher carried out his wish of securing
higher pay for teachers by prescribing under Clause 4 (IV)
of the Regulations for the Supplementary Grants, minimum
salaries for certain grades of teacher at the following
rates (Hansard, 8 May 1917, 904):

Cértificated teachers (men)	£100 per annum
Certificated teachers (women)	£90 per annum
Uncertificated teachers	£65 per annum
Full-time domestic subjects teachers with recognized qualifications	£90 per annum

This intention was carried into effect by a Minute of the
Board dated 14 January 1918.   Circular 1024 explaining the
effect of the Minute was issued to local education

authorities on 22 January 1918.

THE EDUCATION BILL, 1917

On 16 May 1917, Fisher submitted his draft Education Bill
to the War Cabinet for its approval. This was based on
his proposals placed before the Cabinet on 20 February and
centred around four objectives. These were:
   (a)   adequate provision of educational facilities
   (b)   comprehensive provision not only of schools but
         also of scholarships, maintenance allowances and
         the training of teachers
   (c)   co-operation with neighbouring authorities
   (d)   co-ordination of elementary and higher
         education (WCP-O, GT 757, 1917).
In his accompanying, explanatory Memorandum, the President
hoped that the provisions of the Bill, if supported by the
necessary financial support from the Exchequer, would 'go
a long way to promote on broad lines that development of
the public educational system which is generally recognized as essential for the strength and welfare of the
nation' (ibid.).

   In June, the Reconstruction Committee expressed agreement with the general principles of the Education Bill.
It was regarded as a major step forward. But the Committee considered that a system of continuation schools
giving instruction for only eight hours a week was inadequate and uneconomical. The majority of the Committee
recommended that, within five years, a full-time school-
leaving age of 15 and half-time schools up to 18 should
be fully adopted (WCP-O, GT 1304, 1917).

   In June 1917 also Fisher was reporting that the Board
of Education was proceeding with its plans for the
improvement of secondary school examinations and the
formation of a co-ordinating Secondary Schools Examination
Council. A Committee representative of local education
authorities, teachers and others interested in education
had been appointed 'to enquire into the principles which
should determine the construction of scales of salary for
teachers in elementary schools ...' (WCP, GT 902, 1917,
GT 1066, 1917). The local education authorities had been
asked, too, to bring about as close a co-operation as they
could between elementary school teachers and the different
clubs and organizations which endeavoured to promote the
welfare of children out of school hours as well as when
they had left school.

   On 10 August 1917, after receiving the approval of the
War Cabinet and after having sounded out the opinions of

different societies and organizations and receiving
deputations from them at the Victoria and Albert Museum in
Kensington, London, where the Board had moved by June
1917, Fisher introduced his Education Bill in the House of
Commons.

On inspection, the Bill not only revealed that under
its terms the religious settlement of the Balfour Act
would not be amended because the President had no desire
to fan into flames the embers of former religious contro-
versy and wreck the party truce but that the administrative organization would not be altered drastically,
either. The government, however, wished to improve this
machinery by, chiefly, the imposition of a duty on every
county and county borough to provide for the progressive
development and comprehensive organization of education in
their areas by submitting schemes for this purpose to the
Board of Education and by Part II and III authorities co-
operating when reforms were considered.

In addition, the 2d rate limit for higher education in
counties, which had been stipulated under the 1902 Education Act, was removed enabling more advanced academic work
to be undertaken in the schools. Power was also given to
the Board, after consulting the local education authorities concerned, to establish provincial associations to
deal with matters such as higher education and the training of teachers which affected areas covered by more than
one local education authority. Higher education included
secondary education.

The Board was also empowered to make an order providing
for the relinquishing to the county of all, or any, of the
Part III powers and duties of a borough or urban district.
Provision was made for the consolidation of the grants for
elementary education.

Bearing in mind the pleas for more social and educational change which had crescendoed during the twentieth
century, and, too, in Fisher's words, 'to repair the intellectual and physical wastage which had been caused by the
War', the Bill contained clauses dealing with the provision of nursery, elementary and central schools and continuation schools for most young people when they had left
school. Fisher was careful to emphasize in his speech,
however, that the establishment of continuation schools
was the most novel, if not the most important part of the
Bill.

The authority responsible for elementary education was
also encouraged to co-operate with the one accountable for
higher education to ensure the passage of children from
the elementary school to a place of higher education. It
was also to make arrangements for the training and supply

of teachers.

The Bill also included clauses dealing with the abolition of fees in elementary schools; the raising of the
school-leaving age to 14 and to 15 if an authority wished
to do so; the abolition of the half-time employment of
children; medical inspection and treatment of children;
the provision of physical training, holiday or school
camps, playing fields and school baths and the inspection
of schools outside the state sector of education.

Fisher's request for approval from the War Cabinet to
transfer the powers of making by-laws affecting the
employment of children from the Home Office to the Board
of Education had been successful and so there was a clause
in the Bill dealing with this subject (WCP-O, GT 961,
1917). Opposition to this move had come from Sir George
Cave (Unionist, Surrey, Kingston), the Home Secretary
(WCP-O, GT 961a, 1917). The Reconstruction Committee had
supported the substitution (WCP-O, GT 1604, 1917).

Provision was made, as well, for the supply of scholarships and maintenance allowances.

On the same day as the Bill was presented in the
Commons, Colonel Wedgwood (L., Newcastle under Lyme), a
descendant of the famous pottery family, and a member of
Staffordshire County Council from 1910, attacked the Bill
on the grounds that (a) the House of Commons was stale and
out of touch with the constituencies; (b) that the possible loss of wages if certain proposals of the 1917 Bill
were implemented would be too much for those with low
incomes, and that (c) the Bill would bring about a further
restriction in the size of families because they would be
unable to afford them. But F.C. Acland (L., Cornwall
N.W.), a former Examiner in the Education Department, and
the son of A.H. Dyke Acland, formerly Vice-President of
the Council, after he had referred to Wedgwood's attacks
on the Bill as an 'extraordinary refreshing whiff of mid-
Victorian social and political economy', greeted the Bill
as one which would 'mark the greatest advance in the
education of the general people of the country that has
been made since February of 1870, when Mr W.E. Forster
introduced the Education Act'.

The First Reading of the 1917 Bill was soon agreed to
but no further progress was made with it before the House
rose on 21 August 1917. During the Recess, on 24 August
1917, in order to explain those clauses which, in view of
their relation to specific provisions of the existing law
appeared to need special explanation, the Board of Education issued a White Paper entitled 'Notes on Certain
Clauses of the Education Bill, 1917'. Finally, the Bill,
if passed, was to come into force on an 'Appointed Day'.

This was to be fixed by the Board of Education for each of
the many provisions of the Bill and for each area of the
country.

FURTHER REACTIONS TO THE BILL

The reception of the 1917 Education Bill in the country at
the outset was, as in the House of Commons, distinctly
favourable. The professional associations of teachers,
which included the National Union of Teachers, the Incorporated Association of Headmasters, the Headmistresses'
Association, the Association of Assistant Mistresses, the
Incorporated Association of Assistant Masters, the Association of Technical Institutions and the Association of
Teachers in Technical Institutions, as well as the Education Policy Committee of the Headmasters' Association and
the Headmasters' Conference, were content with the Bill.
But attention was drawn to the need for staffing the
continuation schools with men and women of the correct
calibre and for the necessity of considering carefully the
composition of the curriculum in these schools where
accent on purely vocational aspects was deplored.   In
addition, the importance of providing the continuation
schools with adequate space and playing fields was
stressed, as well as the need to control the size of
classes.
    The Private Schools' Association Incorporated (PSAI),
was, however, uneasy about the government's intentions to
encourage the inspection of schools outside the state system because it saw not only the advantages, but the dis-
advantages, even the dangers, which the extension of state
control could bring to it ('Secondary Education', October
1917, 62).
    The churches, on the whole, when they analysed the 1917
Education Bill were not antagonistic to it. They hoped,
however, that the changes proposed would not mean the
large-scale surrender of non-provided schools to the local
education authorities. There was also disquiet that the
increased expenditure needed to provide more advanced and
different work in the elementary schools, central schools
and classes, and more opportunities for children in the
secondary schools, as well as that demanded by the creation of nursery and continuation schools, would place
heavy financial burdens upon them. It worried the
denominations, too, that the compulsory attendance of
young people at continuation schools would mean a burden-
some loss of income for poor families ('Church Times',
August 1917; 'Tablet', August 1917).

The Nonconformists also feared that the establishment of nursery and continuation schools would extend the religious difficulty because they contended that the majority of the schools which would be brought into being would be sectarian ones of the other religious bodies, thus extending the problems of the Dual System when there was a desire to leave it alone ('Christian World', October and November 1917).

Fisher felt, however, that the apprehensions of the Roman Catholics about some parts of the Bill would disappear when they understood it more clearly. If their opposition became serious then he thought this could almost certainly be overcome by a modification of the Board's regulations for secondary schools which had been imposed by R. McKenna when President of the Board of Education 1907-8 (WCP-O, GT 2459, 1917).

The reaction of the Labour movement to the government's 1917 proposals was one of disappointment and the movement regretted that the government had not brought forward a bolder measure. There was pressure for the implementation of the Bradford scheme which had taken up a main point of TUC policy for many years. This meant full-time secondary education up to a leaving age of 16 (PP, Labour Party, 1917).

There was diversity of opinion within the Labour ranks. The Workers' Educational Association, for instance, when it had published its own recommendations for educational reform towards the end of 1916, had suggested that secondary schools should be varied in type. In contrast to the Bradford scheme, it emphasized the need for compulsory part-time education for all children up to 18. Another recommendation was that the school-leaving age should be raised to 15 without exemption within five years but that local authorities should be allowed to make by-laws raising the age to 16 ('TES', 14 December 1916).

While paeans of praise for the 1917 Education Bill came from the majority of the major daily newspapers, immediate hostility, ominously, was expressed by the 'Yorkshire Post' of 11 August 1917. It considered that the cost of implementing the provisions of the Bill would be too exorbitant, both for the nation and the individual family.

The Federation of British Industries, which was founded in mid-1916 not only to encourage, promote and protect industries of all kinds but to express the unified, valuable point of view of industry in the governing councils of the country and whose growth was phenomenal with 890 members by 4 July 1918, also recoiled at some of the provisions in the 1917 Education Bill. These included the setting up of continuation schools, the raising of the

school-leaving age to 14 and possibly to 15 by some
authorities if they wished, and the abolition of the
half-time employment of school children. It was maintained that the implementation of these clauses would dislocate some industries and cause inconvenience to all the
population.

Such views were contained in a letter to Fisher from
the Director of the FBI dated 30 August 1917, enclosing a
copy of a memorandum drawn up by the Education Committee
of the FBI. This had been circulated to members of the
Federation with a questionnaire probing their views about
the proposed reforms in education. In addition, it was
maintained that as a large percentage of children was
incapable of benefiting from education beyond the elementary stage, full-time higher education of a few children
selected as specially fitted for it was more important and
desirable than part-time continuation education for the
many. It was also argued that the implementation of the
continuation school proposals would be impracticable for
some years to come owing to the shortage of teachers and
buildings.

On 31 August 1917, John W. McConnel, Vice-Chairman of
the Fine Cotton Spinners and Doublers' Association Ltd, in
a long and detailed letter to the 'Manchester Guardian',
argued that the reforms of the 1917 Education Bill would
make the spinning and weaving industries of Lancashire and
other counties lose the equivalent of 8 per cent of their
labour force.

The encroaching power of the state was therefore resen-
ted by industrialists, although management was sympathetic
towards state collectivism during wartime in order to wage
the war more successfully. They had also slowly become
accustomed to a certain amount of grouping and association of some trades and industries on a large scale within
their own sector with the corollary of a kind of a central
control by these larger groups. This was in contrast to
much of the laissez-faire policy and smaller units of the
nineteenth century.

The most powerful opposition to the 1917 Education Bill
came from the local education authorities who also feared
its collectivist tendencies. They felt that under certain
of the administrative clauses, such as the procedure for
submitting schemes to the Board of Education for the
reorganization of education in an area, the powers of the
Board (the central authority) would be enlarged at the
expense of those of the local education authorities. The
financial provisions of the government in the 1917 Bill
were also considered unsatisfactory by the local education
authorities. They wanted a minimum government grant of

50 per cent towards educational expenditure. Some, such as the County Councils Association, felt that the grants to local education authorities should amount to not less than 75 per cent of the total cost in respect of education ('TES', 18 October 1917, 400).

The result of the concern felt by the authorities was that they pressured the government through their organizations such as the Association of Education Committees, the County Councils Association, the Association of Municipal Corporations and the Association of Directors and Secretaries of Education during the months following the introduction of the 1917 Bill to have the offending provisions either removed or altered. This was done through meetings, either public or private; through the media of the local and national press, or educational journals; or confrontations with Fisher and his civil servants (in particular Selby-Bigge). The authorities were careful to emphasize, while doing so, that they welcomed the other proposals in the 1917 Education Bill, which, in the struggles that followed, came to be known as the educational provisions (ibid., 11, 18, 25 October 1917).

ACTION BY THE BOARD OF EDUCATION

The outcome was that Fisher and his colleagues at the Board corresponded with, or met, representatives from the different lobbies during the autumn of 1917 to explain the government's intentions in the Education Bill. These included such dignitaries of the Church of England as the Archbishops of Canterbury and York (Drs Randall Davidson and Cosmo Lang), and the Bishop of Manchester (Dr Knox), representing the Church Schools Emergency League; Cardinal Bourne, Mr Anderton of the Catholic Education Council, William O'Dea of the Catholic Teachers' Federation and Archbishop Whiteside of Liverpool for the Catholics, and, of the Free Churches, Dr Scott Lidgett, the Rev. F.B. Meyer, Dr Clifford, Dr Massie of the Congregational Union and delegates from the Wesleyan Methodist Church (WCP, GT 2828, 1917).

In addition to meeting representatives of the local education authorities, Fisher, in an explanatory letter of 24 October 1917 to Cyril Cobb, Chairman of the London Education Committee, in reply to one from Cobb of 22 October 1917 (PP, LCC, 1917), which had requested that the President remove the London Committee's doubts about the administrative clauses of the 1917 Bill, emphasized that it was not the intention of the government through the Bill to roll a 'Juggernaut car' of bureaucracy over the liberties of the local education authorities. The cardinal principle of the 1917 Education Bill, it was pointed out, was that there should be an active and constructive partnership between the central authority and the local education authorities when organizing the service of education. The tendency of the Board's actions, it was contended, had been to give the authorities more freedom by dispensing with tight control, and giving them more responsibility – in short, devolution.

For the government, the kernel of the administrative clauses was the scheme procedure, which, it was also pointed out, had been formally commended by the London County Council in April 1917, and by the Association of Directors and Secretaries, and the Association of Education Officers, thus indicating general agreement. A problem would occur for the government, it was argued, when an authority would not submit a scheme, or persisted in submitting a scheme which the Board of Education could not reasonably approve, or neglected to carry out a scheme which the Board had approved. Something should be done about this, it was contended, because a 'laggard authority' not only inflicted an injustice on the children for whom it was a trustee but was a source of embarrassment to other authorities. It was also a perpetual drag on the maintenance of an adequate national standard of education.

In this connection, when Fisher met a deputation from the Association of Education Committees (led by Dr Brackenbury, also a member of the British Medical Association) on 20 November 1917, he drew attention to the fact that, in 1913-14, seventy-two local education authorities had made no provision for handicraft instruction in elementary schools, twenty-six no arrangements for cookery and other domestic subjects and that laggardliness was not confined to any particular kind of authority ('Schoolmaster', 1 December 1917, 600).

One sequel of the exchange of views and letters by Cobb and Fisher was that copies of both letters were circulated on 25 October 1917 to all chairmen of the Education Committees in England and Wales. This meant that the government's interpretations of the disputed administrative clauses in the 1917 Education Bill were now known to a much wider circle.

FISHER'S TOUR OF THE NORTH AND WEST

As well as conducting his campaign on behalf of the 1917 Bill from London, the President, in order that the principles of the Education Bill should be thoroughly

understood in the country, devoted a large part of the
summer parliamentary recess to touring Lancashire (where
it was accepted by the government that the restrictions
and benefits of the Education Bill would be most directly
felt in the manufacturing districts), Wales, and the
South-West of England (PP, Liberal Party, 1917, 453-93).
On his tour, the President addressed gatherings first
at York on 14 September 1917, then at Sheffield on 15
September. On Tuesday, 25 September, he spoke to a large
audience at the Free Trade Hall in Manchester. It was
here that he refuted McConnel's accusation that the labour
supply in the spinning and weaving industries would be
diminished by 8 per cent by the provisions of the Education Bill (Fisher, 1918, 49f).

He then went on to speak at a prize-giving at Burnley
Municipal Technical School on 27 September 1917, at a
meeting of the Lancashire and Cheshire Institutes at
Rochdale on 28 September and at Liverpool on 2 October
1917. This concluded Fisher's very successful tour in
Lancashire. The War Cabinet took the opportunity shortly
afterwards at one of its gatherings of expressing its
appreciation of the striking success of the President's
meetings (WCP, WC 236(10), 1917).

After this, Fisher addressed audiences in Wales at
Bangor (University College) on 4 October, Swansea on 9
October and Cardiff on 10 October 1917. Here his speeches
were equally successful. He was also impressed by the
enthusiasm of the Welsh people for education.

He then delivered orations at West Country towns such
as Gloucester on 12 October 1917, Bristol on 13 and 14
October and Swindon on 12 November 1917. It was at
Bristol on a Sunday morning that Fisher met the most
enthusiastic audience that he had ever experienced when he
addressed a group of dockers of the Transport and General
Workers' Union hastily gathered together by Ernest Bevin,
the future Labour minister. These dockers rose to their
feet several times during the course of the President's
speech and cheered and waved their handkerchiefs (Fisher,
1940, 106; Bullock, 1960, 85).

It was at Bradford on 2 November 1917, that, impressed
by the representations from the local education authorities that the financial provision in the 1917 Education
Bill would not enable them to carry out the educational
reforms contained in the measure, and having agreed on the
change of policy with the Chancellor of the Exchequer the
previous day, Fisher announced that, under the terms of
the Bill, the authorities would receive a minimum of 50
per cent grant towards the cost of educational expenditure
(Fisher, 1918, 85f). This was an important announcement

because it immediately swept away a difficulty which faced
the authorities. While appreciating it, though, they continued to lobby the Board through their representative
bodies in the period that followed for amendments to the
administrative clauses in the 1917 Bill ('TES', 22 November 1917, 457).

As well as making speeches to explain his plans for
education, Fisher also received deputations, during his
tour of the North and West, from various lobbies. He also
attended policy-influencing meetings. Thus, in the morning of Wednesday, 26 September 1917, in Manchester, he
received representatives of the Federation of Master
Cotton Spinners' Associations and of the Cotton Spinners'
and Manufacturers' Association.

In the afternoon, he attended a very successful reception in the Whitworth Hall at Manchester given by the
General Committee of the Manchester and District Associ-
ated Educational Societies. This gathering included Sir
H. Miers, Vice-Chancellor of Manchester University - whose
name had been floated for the Presidency of the Board of
Education in 1916 - the Bishop, Dean, clergy and university staff ('Manchester City News', 29 September 1917, 5).

The next day, Fisher met representatives of the
Manchester Trades Council and Manchester Labour Party when
a general promise of support for the educational proposals
of the government was given. On Saturday, 29 September,
also in Manchester, the President received deputations
from the cardroom operatives, the Cardroom Amalgamation,
and the Manchester newsagents who interviewed him about
the effects of his plans on paper-selling. While in
Manchester Fisher emphasized that he was actuated by no
unfriendly intentions towards confessional schools when he
met representatives of the Catholic Teachers' Association
('Manchester Guardian', 27 September 1917, 8).

He then lunched with Lancashire teachers at the Midland
Hotel, Manchester. When he addressed, afterwards, a large
meeting of the Lancashire County Association of Teachers
at the Albert Hall in Peter Street, he submitted that he
was desirous, as far as he could, of meeting the views of
the industrial leaders of the county without sacrificing
anything of real value in the Education Bill ('Manchester
City News', 1 October 1917, 8).

Articles in the press at the time mirrored, however,
the conflicting emotions that the Fisher proposals aroused
and the opposition that the President had to fight. Thus
the 'Burnley Express and Advertiser' of 29 September 1917,
following Fisher's visit to Burnley on 27 September, and
other editions, reflected the continuing opposition to,
and sharp criticism of, the 1917 Education Bill, when it

expressed fears over the encroaching power of the Welfare
State and the decline of parental responsibility. The
virtues of Samuel Smiles' 'Self-Help' which, it estimated,
had made the cotton trade of Lancashire and the wealth of
the nation, were also being lost.

Support for the 1917 Education Bill in the Northern
Press at this time, was, however, contained in, for
example, the 'Liverpool Daily Post and Mercury' of 11
August 1917, the 'Manchester City News' of 18 August 1917,
and subsequent editions, the 'Bolton Journal and Guardian'
of 7 September 1917, the 'Rochdale Times' of 29 September
1917 and the 'Bradford Daily Telegraph' of 13 September
1917. The 'TES' of 11 October 1917, moreover, when
reviewing Fisher's campaign in Lancashire, considered that
at Manchester, Liverpool, Rochdale and Burnley the President had pleaded the cause of education in a fashion that
had aroused anew the spirit of the North. Fisher's
felicitous dictum, which he had uttered during his speech
at the Free Trade Hall, Manchester, on 25 September 1917,
that 'Education is the eternal debt which maturity owes to
Youth', was much admired.

THE WITHDRAWAL OF THE 1917 EDUCATION BILL

But the result of the strong criticism of the Education
Bill from some quarters following its introduction on 8
August 1917, in spite of Fisher's energetic defence, was
that its prospects of becoming law by Christmas 1917 began
to dim considerably. On 19 October 1917, Bonar Law,
Leader of the House, announced in the Commons, in answer
to a question from Joseph King (L., Somerset, N.), a barrister, that he feared that it would not be possible to
pass the Bill during the current session. On 22 November
1917, in the House of Lords, Lord Curzon, who was Lord
President of the Council and Leader of the Lords, indicated that the government had no hope of proceeding with the
Bill in that session but intended to give it a very promi-
nent place in the next one.

On 26 November, in a further attempt to save the Bill,
a deputation representing all parties in the Commons met
Lloyd George, Bonar Law and Fisher. They drew from the
Prime Minister an expression of complete sympathy with the
desire of the delegation and also the suggestion, with no
definite pledge, that, if the Parliamentary session were
prolonged, it might be possible to take the Bill towards
the end of it. If not, it would be given priority in the
next session.

But because of the protests about the Board's

intentions of extending its powers over those of the local
education authorities and objections to other portions of
the 1917 Education Bill, and realizing that only an agreed
Bill would pass through Parliament, Bonar Law announced in
the House of Commons on 13 December 1917 that Fisher had
decided to allow the existing Bill to lapse. A new Education Bill which would contain the amendments that Fisher
desired to make to meet the criticisms of the 1917 Education Bill would be introduced. Bonar Law also explained
that the new Education Bill would be taken at the earliest
possible moment in the next session and that the government hoped to pass it without delay.

As an endorsement of this action, the President, in a
letter to 'The Times' on 17 December 1917, explained that
his Education Bill was not dead but that the procedure of
withdrawal and re-introduction was adopted with the object
of saving parliamentary time on its discussion. He also
emphasized that although certain amendments would be made
to meet the apprehensions of the local education authorities, and other bodies there would be no dilution of the
essential principles governing the Bill.

In his Confidential Memorandum on the Education Bill,
1917, to the War Cabinet dated 31 October 1917 Fisher
expressed the fear that unless the government showed that
it wanted to pass the Education Bill 'a suspicion will
arise that the Government is not seriously desirous of
attacking the fundamental problems of reconstruction'
(WCP-O, GT 2459, 1917).

By the end of November 1917, the President had reported
that he had received a number of deputations from bodies
representing the local education authorities about the
administrative clauses of the Education Bill and that, as
a result, he had been able to remove to a very large
extent their objections to the provisions (WCP, GT 2828,
1917).

Amid the consternation and dismay generally in the
country that greeted Bonar Law's announcement in October
1917, with some deriving satisfaction from it, and the
subsequent lack of progress of the Education Bill,
attempts were made in the press to probe the cause of
delay. The agent, in some quarters, was attributed to the
triumph in the War Cabinet of Unionist, Catholic and
Anglican opposition to the Bill. With some, the antagonism of the local education authorities was the true
reason, while, for others, it was the attitude of a substantial manufacturing class which believed that its prosperity was dependent on child labour. Bradford and
Preston were considered regions where local opposition to
the abolition of the half-time employment of children was

strong (WCP-O, GT 2459, 1917).

As the testing year of 1917 drew to a close it seemed that the reactionary movements might prove too strong for the government and its policies for social and educational reform.

Chapter three

New lamps for old –
the Education Act, 1918

THE EDUCATION BILL, 1918

While the Germans were attacking along the Western Front
in their spring offensive of 1918 in a last, despairing
bid to win the war before the starving German nation muti-
nied, the government decided, once again, to introduce
reforming educational legislation.

On 14 January 1918 H.A.L. Fisher brought in under the
ten minutes' rule with G.H. Barnes (Lab., Glasgow, Black-
friars), Stanley Baldwin (Unionist, Worcester, W.), the
future Prime Minister, and Herbert Lewis, his amended
Bill, Education Bill (No. 2). This was read for the
first time.

On examination, it was seen that the 1918 Education
Bill of forty-five.often very long and detailed clauses
covering all aspects of educational provision was substantially the same as the 1917 Education Bill. This
meant, as before, that it was governed by the principle
that as much development in education as possible would
be brought about through the existing structure of education. The Dual System was therefore retained. Encapsulated also in the Bill's proposals were the demands for
social and educational reform which had increased during
the twentieth century and had been accentuated by the
First World War.

While appreciating that the Education Bill introduced
in August 1917 had, in Fisher's words when presenting the
1918 Bill, 'received a remarkable measure of preliminary
benediction and support', it was accepted by the government that the phrasing of some of its administrative
clauses could be interpreted as placing excessive power in
the Board of Education at Whitehall. But it was also felt
that the success of educational development depended far
more upon the partnership between the local education

authorities and the Board than upon the way that their association was worded.

Certain of the administrative clauses of the 1917 Bill were, nevertheless, either absent from the 1918 Bill, or rewritten in such a way that they no longer caused offence to the local education authorities (WCP, GT 3391, 1918). New clauses were thus inserted dealing with the provision of the machinery and procedure for the approval, or dis-approval, of schemes and for the federation, or co-operation, or combination of local education authorities for certain purposes. There were clauses dealing with public enquiries and grants, where provision was made more specifically for a deficiency grant in aid of education in those cases where the substantive grant did not amount to 50 per cent of the approved expenditure of elementary, or higher, education.

Clauses in the 1917 Bill which were not included in the 1918 Bill dealt with the provision of provincial associa-tions, the procedure for the transfer of the powers of non-county boroughs, or urban districts, to the county councils, and the reference to the Board of Education of certain educational questions.

Under the 1918 Bill it was also now the duty of the local education authorities, whether Part II or Part III, in order to establish a national system of education, to provide for the progressive development and comprehensive organization of education in their areas, and, through the submission of schemes to the Board, to show 'the mode in which their duties and powers under the Education Acts are to be performed and exercised, whether separately or in co-operation with other authorities.'

Part III authorities, in order to improve the education in elementary schools and to meet the needs of every kind of child, were to provide central schools, central or special classes, and to include in the curriculum of the elementary schools practical instruction suitable to the ages, capacities and circumstances of the children. These included those aged up to 14 or 15. Advanced instruction for the older, or more intelligent, children, including those who stayed on after the leaving age of 14, was also to be provided. This was to meet the accusations of those who had stated that many children wasted their time in their last years in the elementary school. Fees in elementary schools were abolished, as well.

The government was as anxious to develop opportunities for children to receive a secondary education in the grammar schools as it was to improve elementary education, recognizing that the demand for secondary school places exceeded the supply. Owing, however, to the financial

restrictions which had limited the rate for higher education to 2d, even progressive authorities had only been
able to provide for a minority of children who had wanted
to enter a secondary school following the development of a
municipal system of secondary education after the 1902
Balfour Education Act. With the lifting, under the Fisher
Bill, of the 2d limit of the amount which could be raised
by a county council out of rates for the purpose of education other than elementary, it was hoped that incentive
would be given to Part II local education authorities to
extend the numbers of those receiving it.

A decision, in this connection, that the Lloyd George
Coalition Government had had to make was whether to meet
the demands for full time free secondary education up to
the age of 16, with maintenance allowances, which the
Labour movement, for example, had urged, or whether to
introduce free, day continuation schools. For the government, moreover, the matter could not be argued upon
strictly educational grounds alone because account had to
be taken of industrial conditions. It was maintained,
because of this, that so long as the majority of the population was poor, so the need for the industrial earnings
of children over 14 would continue. The real issue for
the government, therefore, was whether a part-time
continued education, as distinct from elementary education,
or no secondary education at all, was preferable for the
majority of the young people in the country. As Fisher was
to observe later, the government did not consider it suf-
ficient to say that the continuation school was a
cheaper substitute for the secondary school, and that a
full-time secondary education was more desirable than a
part-time continued education (Fisher, 1923b, 443f).

While, therefore, grant-aided secondary schools were
being improved in quality, extended in numbers, and the
total of free places in them being increased, the government wanted the development of continuation schools to
take place, accepting, however, that this would take a
long time and that their creation was not the most press-
ing educational problem facing it.

There was, consequently, in the 1918 Education Bill,
provision for a gradual introduction of a system of free,
compulsory, day continuation classes for young people by
the authorities responsible for higher education in order
to continue their education and help them prepare for
adult life. This was to be for 320 hours in each year, or
the equivalent of eight hours a week for forty weeks, for
those aged 14-18 years, with the young people not having
to attend classes between the hours of 7 p.m. and 2 a.m.
However, after the passing of five years from the

appointed day for the opening of continuation schools, the number of hours of attendance at a continuation school, or any regulations affecting such attendance, could be amended after consultation between the Board of Education and the local education authority. A young person, furthermore, could claim exemption from the obligation to attend continuation classes, if, for example, he had passed the matriculation examination of a university of the United Kingdom, or an examination recognized by the Board of Education as its equivalent. Nor was he under any obligation to attend a continuation school if, for instance, he could show to the satisfaction of the local education authority that he was under full-time instruction in a school recognized by the Board of Education as efficient, or to be under suitable and efficient full-time instruction in some other way.

Employers were also encouraged to recognize their educational responsibilities towards their employees by establishing part-time day continuation schools in their firms, thus rejecting any leanings towards evening class instruction. But the consent of a young person was needed if he were required by a local education authority to attend any continuation school held at, or in connection with, the place of his employment. He had, also, as far as practicable, to be given a choice of schools.

It was decreed, as well, in the 1918 Bill, that young persons who had to attend continuation classes should not work long hours during the days on which classes would be held, and should have a reasonable interval in which to eat, rest and wash between work and school. Classes were not to be held on a Sunday, nor on any day, nor part of a day, which was set aside for religious services by the religious body to which a young person belonged. Neither were classes to be held on any holiday, or half-holiday, which the young people were accustomed to enjoy.

The aim, when the content of the curricula which would be taught in the schools was considered, was that a general education would be provided which would build on the foundations laid in the elementary school. This had been outlined by Fisher on 10 August 1917 when introducing the 1917 Education Bill in the Commons. Some vocational bias would be given to the instruction in the schools, which would be graded according to the age and occupation of the pupil, with courses varying from locality to locality, and with those given in the rural districts not being identical with those in the towns. The basic conception of the continuation scheme would, however, be the same over the whole country. This would be the production of suitable citizens able to make the most of themselves and of the environment in which they were placed.

Physical education, furthermore, would be a part of the instruction because it was considered that it was important for boys and girls to be physically fit. It was hoped that closer links would be formed between continuation schools and the increasing number of voluntary societies helping the needs of young people, such as Boys' and Girls' Clubs and Brigades, Boy Scouts, Girl Guides, and other associations.

When dealing with the provision of schools, in the new Bill as in the old one, local education authorities were empowered to supply, or aid the supply of, nursery schools for children over 2 and under 5, or a later age if approved by the Board of Education, if attendance at such schools was necessary, or desirable, for the 'healthy physical and mental development' of the children. Such arrangements had to bear in mind the industrial and housing conditions in an area.

In order to improve the lives of school children, exemptions from attending schools between the ages of 5 and 14 were abolished. This meant the abandonment of the half-time system of employment, the raising of the school-leaving age to 14 and to 15, by by-law, if a local authority so desired.

Further restrictions placed upon the out-of-school employment of children meant that children up to the age of 14 could not be employed on any day in which they were required to attend school before the close of school hours on that day, nor on any day before 6 a.m. nor after 8 p.m. This regulation amended the Employment of Children Act, 1903, the Factory and Workshop Acts 1901-11, the Coal Mines Act, 1911. and the Metalliferous Mines Acts, 1872 and 1875. It affected children employed in street trading, in factories, workshops, mines and quarries.

Under the 1918 Bill, moreover, no child before 12 could be employed for the purpose of singing, playing or performing, or be exhibited for profit, or offer anything for sale. Children under 14 could not be employed for the purpose of doing the same things before 8 p.m. Furthermore, licences for the employment of children to perform could not be obtained before the age of 12. These provisions amended the Prevention of Cruelty to Children Act, 1904, as far as it related to England and Wales.

Another feature of the 1918 Education Bill was that medical inspection and treatment was to be provided in all schools maintained by every local education authority. Close attention, too, was to be paid by local education authorities to the social and physical training provided in schools, including educational institutions for those

over 18. This provision in the Bill included holiday or
school camps, especially for young persons attending
continuation schools; centres and equipment for physical
training, playing fields (in addition to the ordinary
playgrounds in elementary schools), school baths and
school swimming baths, as well as facilities for social
and physical training in the day or evening. Attention to
the physical welfare of children and young people was thus
a distinctive feature of both Bills.

If any school or educational institution not liable to
inspection by any government department requested the
Board of Education to inspect the school or institution
and give a report then the Board could do so, if they
wanted to, free of cost. In order, also, that full information would be available to the Board of Education about
the provision of education, and the use of such provision
in England and Wales, all schools and educational institutions not in receipt of grants from the Board of Education
were asked to supply the Board with the name and address
of the school or institution, together with a short des-
cription of the school or institution.

In addition there were clauses in the Bill dealing with
the supply and training of teachers by the local education
authorities, the appointment of teachers of secular subjects, the closure and grouping of schools, the distribution of children between schools, the appointment of
managers in elementary schools and the provision of premises for classes in practical or advanced instruction.

Some clauses dealt also with the compulsory purchase of
land by local education authorities to carry out their
duties, the siting of elementary schools and the expenses
incurred by a council in carrying out the Education Acts.
The power to prosecute any person who was cruel to children was included, too.

Others covered public enquiries held by the Board of
Education, the signing of documents by a local education
authority, educational trusts, assurance, and educational
charities and trustees.

Explaining in the Commons when he introduced the 1918
Education Bill that he had placed a new Bill before the
House containing amendments which had been requested of
him, instead of delaying any desirable changes until the
Committee stage of the Bill, Fisher hoped that this would
expedite discussion of the Bill in Committee, although he
did not want to withdraw from MPs the opportunity of dis-
cussing fully the Education Bill. A new White Paper
entitled 'Notes on the Education (No.2) Bill, 1918' outlining the changes of substance was introduced.

With the Parliamentary Session coming to an end on

6 February 1918, a fresh Bill was introduced in the new
session and given a First Reading, without discussion, on
25 February 1918. Identical with the No.2 Bill except for
some small drafting additions, it came to be known as the
Education (No.3) Bill, 1918 (BEP, 1900, 1918).

REACTIONS TO THE BILL

Close interest in the 1918 Education Bill, both inside and
outside Parliament, was taken when it was introduced. In
the debates in Parliament (Appendix C), support or opposition from the doves or hawks for certain sections of the
Bill sometimes cut across party affiliations.
     Fisher subsequently expressed disappointment at the
assistance that he received from Labour MPs, submitting
that they passed resolutions at party conferences which
were not upheld in Parliament. F.W. Goldstone (Lab.,
Sunderland), an official of the NUT, was excepted from
this criticism. Fisher found that a Tory like Lord Henry
Cavendish Bentinck gave him more assistance in the House.
The President also felt that ex-half-timers and ex-pupil
teachers like J.R. Clynes (Lab., Manchester, N.E.),
Secretary of the Lancashire District of the National Union
of General Workers and President of the Council of the
Union, and Philip Snowden (Soc., Blackburn), a journalist,
Chairman of the Independent Labour Party 1903-6 and later
Labour Minister, preferred the system under which they had
been educated (Fisher, 1940, 110f). The attitude of some
Labour MPs may have been due to the fact that they did not
consider the Bill was radical enough.
     The local education authorities, which had fought so
determinedly to halt the invasion of the Board of Education on their territory, soon expressed their satisfaction
over the amendments to the administrative clauses. They
promised support for the 1918 Bill, as Fisher had hoped,
although there were murmurings that the 50 per cent grant
should be raised to 75 per cent (CCA, 'Gazette', December
1917, 130).
     In Parliament, on 13 March 1918, during the Second
Reading of the Bill, this agreement between the authorities and the government was expressed by MPs such as Sir
Henry Hibbert (Unionist, Lancashire, N. Chorley), a flour
merchant, member of the Manchester Exchange, Chairman of
the Education Committee of the Lancashire County Council,
and Chairman of the Education Committee of the County
Councils Association, who had taken part in the discussions with Fisher and his colleagues, and Sir Willoughby
H. Dickinson (L., St Pancras, N.), a former member of the

London Education Committee. However, on the same day, regret for the government's action came from F.C. Acland, who had quickly praised the 1917 Bill, and who would have preferred wider powers being given to the Board of Education. In the Lords on 24 July 1918, Lord Haldane, who had long favoured the creation of provincial associations, preferred the original intentions of the government.

Under Clauses 4 and 6 of the 1918 Education Bill, however, the powers and duties of the local education authorities were markedly extended, with the powers of co-operation between the Part II and Part III authorities being consolidated and enlarged by the formation, if desired, of joint committees. The establishment of federations of local education authorities, or 'provinces', to deal with matters of mutual interest could also take place. This was especially so in the realm of higher education when dealing, for example, with the training of teachers and higher technical education. These delegated bodies did not have the power to levy a rate, or borrow money.

The professional associations of teachers also welcomed the new Education Bill because of the attention directed to the supply and training of teachers. They felt, too, that the financial arrangements in it would not only help local education authorities to carry out the reforms that were needed but also to pay adequate salaries to the teachers in a more satisfactory way. The unions had not been pleased with the way that many local education authorities had used the money from the 1917 Supplementary Grant to relieve local rates, instead of increasing the salaries of teachers on the scales prescribed by Fisher on 8 May 1917, on the ground that an opportunity was being lost of making teaching a worthwhile profession. The National Association of Head Teachers, for example, at its 21st Annual Conference at Bradford in May 1918, drew attention to the fact that in Manchester, where the Supplementary Grant amounted to £90,000, only £45,000 had been spent upon the salaries of teachers; that in Halifax, the teachers had received £4,000 from a grant of £13,000, while Leeds had paid £36,000 out of £56,000 in increased salaries. It caused the Association concern that, while 3,000 fully certificated men teachers received less than £100 per annum, fewer than 100 teachers received £400 a year, and only two received salaries of between £400 and £500 per annum ('Education', 31 May 1918, 233).

Support in the Commons, to improve the numbers, pay and conditions of service of the teachers, came from Sir Henry Craik (Unionist, Glasgow and Aberdeen Universities), Secretary of the Scottish Education Department, 1885-1904,

who observed during the Second Reading of the 1918 Education Bill on 13 March 1918 that people assumed that the
teaching profession had to 'consist of people who were a
sort of animated missionaries filled with an enthusiasm
which could do without the ordinary sustenance which is
commonly given to members of other professions', and,
quoting Sir Walter Scott, that the country had 'treated
the schoolmaster as we would treat the deerhound. We have
kept him starved that he may be more alert to bring down
the quarry.' In the Lords, on 23 July 1918, Lord Gainford
(formerly J.A. Pease, President of the Board of Education,
1911-15), and who had hoped to introduce an Education Bill
in 1914, supported this theme.

Bearing all shades of opinion in mind, at its Conference at Bradford in May 1918, the Head Teachers' Association passed a resolution that no educational reform would
be effective which did not make ample provision for a
supply of adequately remunerated teachers but it was not
prepared to go further. A motion which favoured salaries
becoming a charge on the state as a way of removing the
difficulties which arose when they depended upon the rates
was defeated by a very large majority because some delegates feared that this would mean a loss of freedom for
the teachers (ibid.).

Fisher at this time also rejected the possibility of
making teachers civil servants because he thought that it
would endanger educational freedom, curtail experiment and
local responsibility and thus take control by the Board
too far (Fisher, 1940, 97).

Equal pay for men and women teachers was not accepted,
either, at this time, although the large female membership
of the NUT and the women's unions, such as the Association
of Headmistresses, the Association of Assistant Mistresses
and the National Federation of Women Teachers pressed for
it. J.A. Whitehouse attempted, unsuccessfully, on 3 July
1918, during the Committee stage of the Bill, to introduce
a new clause (Teachers' Salaries), which would have
ensured that women teachers received the same pay as men
for equal work.

The Lower Houses of Convocation of Canterbury and York
expressed agreement with the revised Education Bill. The
National Society welcomed the attention that had been paid
to its amendments to the 1917 Education Bill which the
Archbishop of Canterbury, Dr Randall Davidson, had submitted on its behalf. These included references to the
provision of secular education, general protection of
voluntary schools from an unfriendly Board of Education
and councils bearing in mind any existing supply of efficient and suitable non-provided schools or colleges when

preparing schemes. Facilities to enable a child to
receive religious instruction, as well as secular instruction, were afforded in the 1918 Education Bill.

The Nonconformists, while remaining uneasy over the
establishment of denominational nursery and continuation
schools, felt that the new Bill had dispelled many of
their fears.

The apprehensions of the Roman Catholics about the
government's intentions continued to be expressed when
amendments to the 1918 Bill, which came to be known as
the Bishops' 18 Points, based on suggestions presented to
them by the Executive Committee of the Catholic Education
Council, were published in February 1918 by the Roman
Catholic Bishops. These centred around the question of
parental rights; the claim of denominational bodies to
provide and have maintained as part of the national system
both elementary and other confessional schools; the non-
transference of children from one school to another without parental consent and the safeguarding of the privilege
of supplying and training denominational teachers.

THE COST OF EDUCATIONAL REFORM

Inevitably when the Bill was analysed, as with the 1917
Bill, there was the accusation that the government had no
mandate from the electorate to introduce a major, reforming Education Bill in wartime. Sir F. Banbury, for
example, during the Second Reading in the Commons on 13
March 1918, in hawkish mood, did not consider it a practicable proposition, when the country was spending £6-7
million daily on the war, and when there was already a
National Debt of £6,000 million, which would amount to
£8,000 million if the war went on for another year, to
inflict upon the taxpayer and ratepayer an unknown expenditure. In addition, J.A.R. Marriott (Oxford), the well-
known historian, wanted to know, on 18 March 1918, if
there was any estimate of the cost which the removal of
the 2d limit would cause.

Very conscious of the cost of educational reform and
the danger of attempting too much in too many directions
at once, with the possibility that nothing would be accomplished and the whole movement of educational reform would
be put in disrepute, Fisher's explanation of the government's standpoint on the financial issue during the Second
Reading of the 1918 Bill on 13 March 1918 hinged on the
fact that anything in the nature of an exact estimate of
the cost of the education proposals was impossible at that
stage because it would be very difficult to gauge the

extent to which local education authorities might take
advantage of their new powers. Nobody could forecast the
price of building material during the ten years following
the conclusion of the war.

Attempting a rough estimate of the cost of some of the
leading provisions in the Bill, it was submitted that the
cost of raising the school-leaving age to 14 would amount
to £1 million annually, and the cost of the proposals for
continuation education, assuming that the size of classes
was limited to thirty children, would amount to
£8,750,000 a year. Quoting an estimate which had been
submitted to the Manchester local education authority, an
urban community of 716,000, for providing compulsory part-
time education for young people between the ages of 14 and
18, the President explained that in the first year this
cost was calculated at £10,000, in the second, £14,000, in
the third, £21,000, and in the fourth, £28,000. It was
emphasized, however, that the authorities would receive
back part of this in grants from the state. An estimate
for the total eventual cost, to be divided between rates
and taxes, of the provision of nursery schools which was
not compulsory, might, moreover, amount to £900,000.

Calculating from available figures, J.H. Lewis, on 18
March 1918, during the Second Reading of the Bill, drew
attention to the fact that it would cost the Exchequer
about £850,000 to bring the grants for elementary education up to 50 per cent of the expenditure in those areas
where they fell below that standard and that in the case
of higher education it would cost about £265,000 to bring
the grants up to 50 per cent.

The clauses dealing with the system of percentage
grants to meet the expenditure of the local education
authorities, and the removal of the 2d limit, were, in
spite of the anxiety at the cost of the education proposals, eventually carried.

SECONDARY EDUCATION

The cost of educational reform was queried on 7 May 1918,
during the Committee stage of the 1918 Bill, when the provision of secondary education was debated. Some members,
such as J.H. Whitehouse, F.W. Goldstone and Joseph King,
in order to create a national system of education and
eliminate a class structure, pressed for either a complete
arrangement of free secondary education, or at least 25
per cent of free places in grammar schools. Even free
university education was mentioned.

Because of the possible exorbitant cost, Sir F. Banbury

could not agree to a considerable enlargement of secondary education. R. McKenna (L., Monmouthshire, N.), a former President of the Board of Education, while desirous that children who wanted a free secondary education should receive it, also advised MPs not to press Fisher too far because there would not be enough teachers, buildings and equipment to create an entirely new system of education. The President had to build on the existing system and could not scrap it. Another MP, Sir Montague Barlow (Unionist, Salford, S.), a barrister, thought that the ideal of providing free secondary education for all was commendable but impracticable at that time. Major Edward Wood (Unionist, Yorkshire, W.R., Ripon), Fisher's successor at the Board of Education in the Conservative government, stressed that there was no demand for more secondary education and that those who asked for it were not 'representing ordinary, normal, everyday lay opinion' outside the House.

Fisher, on this issue, while accepting that there was an inadequate provision of free places in secondary schools and hoping that there would be more in the future, as well as being cost conscious, argued that the most effective way of producing more secondary education was to encourage local education authorities to build more secondary schools. They should then apply for grants in respect of these schools. This would, in turn, enable them to provide more free places in the schools. These should be varied according to industrial and social conditions.

No reason was seen, either, for abolishing the system of school fees for attendance at these schools because the loss of revenue to the state would be about £1,200,000 which the Exchequer could not afford. It was thus considered reasonable that fees should be paid if parents could afford them.

On the provision of secondary education, Fisher drew attention to the fact that under Clauses 1 and 2 of the Bill more of this could be provided because a duty was imposed on the county boroughs and county councils to provide such forms of secondary education in their areas which would enable all children, whatever their capabilities, to profit from it. Authorities responsible for further and elementary education were to ensure that children were able, at suitable ages, to transfer from the elementary school to a school in higher education. Any scheme submitted to the Board of Education, in this connection, which did not in the opinion of the Board make adequate provision for secondary education in its area, with free places, would be condemned.

Later, in order to impress on the local education
authorities their duties, a sub-section to Clause 4 of the
1918 Bill was inserted to the effect that, as far as practicable, when they drew up their schemes, by the provision
of maintenance allowances, children and young people would
not be debarred from the benefits of higher education,
however poor they might be.

CONTINUATION SCHOOLS

As well as the concern at the possible cost of implementing the proposals of the 1918 Education Bill, the alarm of
the encroaching power of the state, with, it was argued, a
loss of freedom for organizations, parents and children,
was a recurring theme, with variations, both inside and
outside Parliament, during the discussions on the Bill.
Such debate occurred over proposals like the creation of
nursery schools, the raising of the school-leaving age,
the strength-sapping half-time employment of school children, medical inspection and treatment for children, the
abolition of fees in elementary schools, the provision of
playing fields, school baths, swimming baths, holiday or
school camps and centres and equipment for physical
training, the inspection of schools outside the state
system and the employment of school children.
     Fisher and his supporters not only attempted to allay
fears in this direction in Parliament but also met representatives, such as those from the milk trade and the
newspaper business, who felt that their trade would be
affected if the employment of children were curtailed.
In this connection, delegates were seen from the Manchester and District Newsagents' Protection Society, the
Weekly Newspaper and Periodical Proprietors' Association,
the London and Provincial Retail Newsagents', Booksellers'
and Stationers' Association, the Newspaper Conference, the
United Kingdom Federation of Retail Newsagents and Associations representing the whole of the Retail and Wholesale
Newspaper Trade and the London Retail Dairymen's Association (BEP, 1900, 1918).
     The President also met members of the Actors' Associ-
ation, the Provincial Entertainments Proprietors' and
Managers' Association and the Theatrical Managers' Association. In April 1918, a deputation, which he found very
erratic, including Miss Italia Conti, who acted as secretary, Sir Johnston Forbes Robertson, Sir Arthur Pinero,
H.B. Irving, Henry Arthur Jones and Gerald du Maurier,
argued that five plays could not be acted if the 1918
Education Bill became law because there would not be

enough young actors and actresses to play the parts.
Fisher was disappointed with the attitude of the acting
profession towards the Bill as he wrote in his diary (PP,
Fisher, 1918). He felt it was not understood. The President's reaction reveals the strain that a Minister can be
under when piloting an important Bill through Parliament.

The government's measures affecting the employment of
children were, however, with minor amendments, carried.

It was over the proposals to improve the educational
facilities for young people when they had left school by
creating continuation schools that the accusation was most
forcibly heard, during the debates on the 1918 Education
Bill, from lobbies both inside and outside Parliament,
that the state was encroaching too much upon the freedom
of the individual; that parental authority over children
up to the age of 18 was being practically abolished and
that the Board of Education had been set up in its place.
This feeling linked up with the fears that had been
aroused in some by continuation school proposals from the
very beginning when it had been felt that with their creation the German socialism of the Bismarckian welfare state
would be introduced into Britain. The vast Krupps munition compound at Essen where the hard-working lives of the
employees were controlled from an early age, with every
amenity being provided, was taken as an example. This was
in addition to the anxiety aroused during the twentieth
century by German industrial, military and naval power.
B.E. Peto, the Conservative MP for Wiltshire, East, and a
director of Morgan Crucible Co. Ltd, Battersea, London, in
the Commons, for instance, cried, during the Second Reading of the 1918 Bill, on 13 March 1918, 'We are fighting
this War against Prussianism, and I do not think that the
people when they understand this Bill will be willing to
entrust the right hon. Gentleman with powers to set up a
latter day Star Chamber in respect of those young persons,
as he calls them, and their parents.'

In addition to the apprehension expressed in Parliament, the Roman Catholics continued to demand, over the
provision of continuation schools, that there should be no
undue interference with the essential rights of parents;
that they should be able to provide their own continuation
schools and to obtain the removal of the compulsory elem-
ent from the proposals for continuation schools. These
requests were conveyed in meetings and letters between the
Board, and, for instance, Cardinal Bourne and Mr Anderton;
in the publication of the Roman Catholic Bishops' 18
points in February 1918; by amendments pressed in the
House of Commons by Catholic MPs such as Sir Mark Sykes
(Unionist, Hull, Central), Assistant Secretary of the War

Cabinet 1917, and by the hundreds of printed postcards of
protest sent by the Catholic soldiers serving in the
trenches to Parliament.

The Nonconformists also through such people as Dr Scott
Lidgett, and Dr Massie on behalf of the Education Committee of the Congregational Union, continued to communicate
their alarm at the prospect of continuation (and nursery)
schools being run by the denominations and receiving
public money to do so.

The very powerful industrial lobby persisted with its
objections to the proposals for continuation schools,
which had been heard after the introduction of the 1917
Education Bill, on the grounds that they would be impracticable to work, would dislocate industry and would cause
hardship. It had been anticipated by concerned specta-
tors, however, that the main danger to the 1918 Education
Bill would come from this opposition of a powerful group
of employers who were determined to retain child labour
for the industry in which they were interested ('TES',
28 February 1918, 95; 'The Times', 26 February 1918, 7).

The viewpoint of industrial interests was communicated
to Fisher on 11 January 1918 when the Director of the
Federation of British Industries sent him a copy of the
FBI's famous Memorandum whose recommendations had been
carefully compiled from the replies of over 2,000 firms
to the memorandum and questionnaire on education which
had been circulated in August 1917 to members of the newly
created Federation and affiliated associations. This
Memorandum not only condemned the government's proposals
for the creation of continuation schools but felt that
there was a genuine danger that the country might be carried beyond the bounds of practical good sense by the
rush of enthusiasm for social reform which industry considered had been one of the products of the spiritual
upheaval caused by the war. The question was therefore
raised as to whether the government's proposals for educational reform were not an example of this tendency.
Welcoming the ideas behind the 1918 Education Bill, the
Federation nevertheless wondered, also, if it was not
really an attempt to force upon the country a scheme which
neither the educational, nor the economic system, was suf-
ficiently developed to support. It wondered if the
country was going to repeat the mistake of 1870 and
inaugurate a vast programme of educational reform before
it had the necessary quality and quantity of teachers to
carry it out.

The Federation's own ideas for educational reform in
the Memorandum remained centred around the need to adapt
education to the requirements of the industries which

would, after the end of the war, be in the greatest need
of the best brains which the country could provide; to
improve the elementary education of all children and to
select the most promising material from among these children, say at the age of 12, and concentrate the maximum of
educational effort upon them. A similar selection procedure was to be applied at 18 for those who wanted to
receive a university education.

Fisher's response to the Memorandum, and to a delegation from the FBI on 6 February 1918, whose spokesmen were
F.W. Gilbertson of the South Wales Sheet Metal Trade, and
the ubiquitous J.W. McConnel, who, as has been seen, had
expressed his disquiet over the 1917 Education Bill, was
to point out, among many observations, that he had to
approach the problem of educational reform from the
national rather than from the merely industrial standpoint. The provision of continuation schools would,
therefore, be of considerable assistance to industry
because they would provide a moral and social supervising
agency over adolescents. This should go far to counteract
the growing indiscipline among young workers whose minds
were often full of nothing but industrial grievances (BEP,
1900, 1918).

The determination of the FBI to offer serious opposition to the 1918 Education Bill, and in particular to the
proposals for providing continuation schools, clarified
during February 1918 when a special committee of the
Federation was appointed to prepare amendments which were
to be pressed with all possible force during the Committee
stage of the 1918 Bill in Parliament in an attempt to
whittle down the requirements for compulsory day continuation schools ('TES', 28 February 1918, 95). The object of
the amendments was, first, to remove the requirements for
continuation education altogether, and then, if these
efforts failed, to attempt to limit the continuation proposals by granting exemption to young people in certain
industries, or by reducing the hours of attendance a week
to eight, four or even two.

In addition to the antagonism by the FBI to the government's educational proposals, dissatisfaction at this time
about the continuation school provisions within the cotton
industry was expressed by such bodies as the Employers'
and Operatives' Associations; the General Council of the
United Textile Factory Workers' Association; the Legislative Council of the United Textile Workers' Federation;
the Federation of Master Cotton Spinners' Association;
the Cotton Spinners' Manufacturers' Association and the
Master Spinners' Federation, who either wrote to Fisher
and his officials, or sent deputations.

Such lobbies as the Shipbuilding Employers' Federation;
the Mining Association of Great Britain; the Miners'
Federation; the Engineers; the National Federation of
Building Trades Employers and the Institute of Builders
also used similar tactics.

After earlier doubts, the Agricultural Education Association eventually sent a resolution to the President firmly
supporting the 1918 Education Bill. It expressed the hope
that when it was finally adopted it might enable children
in rural schools to obtain vocational training in rural
interests.

Several Manchester firms during this period were anti-
cipating the proposals for continued education by providing facilities for their junior employees to attend the
commercial arithmetic, book-keeping, business routine,
language, shorthand and secretarial classes which had been
organized at the new municipal high school of commerce.
A number of employees had also been allowed to take up
matriculation courses, when groups of twenty or thirty
pupils had been sent by firms during two or three half-
days a week on full pay with, in addition, the employers
paying the school fees.

The firm of Messrs Fletcher, Burrows & Co, of Atherton,
whose collieries were considered to be models because of
their comfortable working conditions, expressed the
opinion that a reduction of working hours in cotton factories would be beneficial to the cotton trade and to the
workers.

The major cotton manufacturing firm of Tootal Broad-
hurst, Lee & Co. also showed its support for the 1918 Bill
by publishing in the press during March 1918, on its own
initiative, and at its own expense, a series of four
advertisements firmly upholding the provisions in the Bill
as it stood, and pointing out the national importance of
the measure. This firm set up a day continuation school
on the lines suggested in the Education Bill as a practical demonstration of what could be done in the cotton
industry.

Such firms as the British Westinghouse Electrical
Manufacturing Co. at Trafford Park, Manchester, Cadbury
at Bourneville, Boots of Nottingham, Rowntree of York and
Crosse & Blackwell of London, had either established
schools, following the example of the Admiralty, which,
since 1843, had organized part-time day schools for dock-
yard apprentices, or had allowed their young employees to
attend school during the daytime.

THE CAMPAIGN AGAINST THE PROVISION OF CONTINUATION SCHOOLS

The outcome of industry's decision either to eliminate
completely the continuation school proposals in the 1918
Education Bill, or to have them considerably modified, was
that a group formed in the House of Commons for this purpose led by Sir Henry Hibbert. This was subsequently
known as the Lancashire group and repeatedly and force-
fully drew attention to the dislocation which would be
caused in industry if young people were to be employed on
a part-time basis without, it seemed to them, gaining much
educational benefit from their visits to the schools.

The result was that not only did Hibbert and his supporters attack the government's intentions but put forward
counter-proposals during the Second Reading on 13 March
1918 and the Committee stage on 30 May 1918 of the 1918
Bill. One of these, briefly, provided for a complete
system of half-time education from 14 to 16, instead of
the government's 320 hours a year from 14 to 18, and
another allowed for different systems of continuation
education. This placed the onus of decision on the local
education authorities as to whether they should use the
government's plan or Hibbert's amendments.

Fisher, however, was unable on 5 June 1918 to accept
the Hibbert options, mainly because he could not see how
a half-time system could be established between the ages
of 14 and 16 without causing industrial disturbance and
dislocation in the labour market, together with a loss of
industrial wages which it would be unfair to ask the
country to pay. Another reason was that the existence of
two or more systems would be too complex to administrate.

Influenced, however, by considerations not only for
the textile industry but of the other lobbies which had
contacted him, Fisher, during the Committee stage of the
Bill on 5 June 1918, made his unexpected concessions. He
argued that while he had been unable to accept Hibbert's
amendments he was prepared to accept modifications to his
own proposals which would, he believed, be more to the
advantage of industrial interests than even Hibbert's
suggestions.

The effect of these modifications was that the obligation to attend continuation schools for young people between the ages of 16 and 18 would not come into operation
until seven years from the appointed day on which the
continuation school provisions came into force, nor after
this period for any young person who had attained the age
of 16 before the expiration of it. The hours of attendance for young people between 14 and 16 would be limited
to 320 hours, but if, during the initial period of seven

years, the local education authorities so decided, the
number of hours for which a young person might be
required to attend continuation schools in any year could
be 280 instead of 320.

Fisher's reason for making his concessions was that no
great harm would result from them so long as Parliament
agreed to the principle that the system of continuation
schools, with all its unquestioned moral, intellectual and
physical benefits would sooner or later be extended over
the whole country. On the contrary, he urged that the
interval between the completion of the first stage and its
further extension would have the advantage of enabling
more careful preparation to be given both to the provision
of buildings and training teachers for the schools.

Fisher's action aroused comment from many sources but
he was no trimmer and he was subsequently to point out
that if a Minister wishes to pilot a Bill through Parliament he must be prepared to make concessions. They seemed
large at the time, he was to admit, but he submitted that
in reality they were of little practical importance since
several years would have been needed before an adequate
supply of efficient teachers would have been forthcoming.
If he had not made the concession, moreoever, to postpone
for seven years the application of his scheme for compulsory part-time continuation schools for young people between 16 and 18 in order to overcome the resistance of the
Lancashire MPs and industrial interests, then Fisher
thought that the 1918 Education Bill would not have
reached the statute book (Fisher, 1940, 108).

Among the stunned observations in the Commons on 5 June
1918 that followed the announcement of the government's
changes, Asquith regretted them, although prepared to
accept them and so far as his opinion was of any value to
recommend the House to accept them. Ramsay Macdonald
(Socialist and Labour, Leicester), the future Labour
Prime Minister, preferred Hibbert's 14-16 alternative to
Fisher's compromise, while F.W. Goldstone, although understanding the President's predicament, felt disappointed
at his capitulation. J.H. Whitehouse regretted, too, that
vested interests had compelled the government to make such
drastic changes.

Some Lancashire MPs, such as L.F. Scott, the Unionist
Member for Liverpool Exchange, a barrister, and Sir N.W.
Helme (L., Lancashire, N.), a manufacturer and JP for the
county of Lancaster, opposed Hibbert's thinking believing
that continued education up to the age of 18 would be of
considerable advantage to the country, while Walter Runciman, who had introduced his ill-fated School and Continuation Class Attendance Bill in 1911, agreed with the

concessions.

The closing stages of this critical debate on Fisher's far-reaching proposals to provide some form of education in school for those young people who had left it, when Sir Henry Hibbert subsequently withdrew his amendments and those of the government were accepted, had been a testing time for the President. As the interest in the arguments had been so intense on 4-5 June 1918 the 11 o'clock rule had been suspended and the Commons had debated until 1.30 a.m. Fisher summed up the occasion by writing in his diary for Wednesday, 5 June 1918, that it was a very disagreeable debate with his friends turning on him for the concessions (PP, Fisher, 1918).

OTHER REACTIONS TO THE FISHER AMENDMENTS

Outside Parliament, the government's concessions over the continuation school proposals were received without enthusiasm in many quarters but defended in others. The 'Westminster Gazette', for example, of 6 June 1918, came out with a sober article under the heading 'The Ulster of Education' - which referred to Lancashire - and deeply regretted the withdrawals, concessions and evasions of the government. Fisher's reply to these criticisms in an interview with a representative of the 'Observer' of 9 June 1918 made this paper admit that the President's defence was reassuring, although it considered that the scheme for continuation education could have been worked out in less time than seven years.

George Cadbury, whose continuation school at the Cadbury works at Bourneville, Birmingham, had been visited by Fisher in February 1918 congratulated the President on the wisdom of the government's action. He agreed that it would have been impossible to have obtained enough teachers or buildings all at once (BEP, 1900, 1918).

The FBI also welcomed the government's concessions because of its contention that there would be a shortage of teachers and building accommodation after the war to implement the continuation school proposals and because industry would have the opportunity of adjusting itself to the new arrangements (PP, CBI, 1918).

The Jewish Church, too, was satisfied with the final shape of the continuation school proposals because it exempted Jewish children from attending continuation classes on Sabbaths and holy days ('Jewish Chronicle', 1918).

A similar, pleased, reaction came from the National Committee on Sea Training because any young person who had

completed satisfactorily a course of training for, and was
engaged in, the sea service in accordance with the provisions of a national scheme formed to maintain an adequate supply of well-trained British seamen - which was an
important consideration at this time when so much reliance
was placed upon seapower - should also be exempted from
compulsory continuation education. Fears had been
expressed that continuation education would cut down the
supply of young recruits for the Royal Navy and Mercantile
Marine whose age of entry for boys was, respectively, $15\frac{1}{4}$
and $15-15\frac{1}{2}$ (BEP, 1900, 1918).

But disappointment over the continuation school concessions was expressed by the teachers' unions because considerable importance had been attached by them to the need
to retain young people in the care and guidance of the
teacher during the impressionable period between 14 and
18. The NUT, for example, had been further disturbed by
the Hibbert amendments because it had felt that if the
'stop-at-16' suggestion had been adopted it would have
been many years before the next step to 18 would have been
taken. It based its fears on the fact that it had taken
so long to abolish the half-time employment of children
('Schoolmaster', 23 March 1918, 359). The difficulties
with which Fisher had had to contend and the solution of
them, were, however, understood by all unions.

The Workers' Educational Association, in similar vein,
although considering that the 1918 Education Act was
weaker than the 1917 Bill, argued that Fisher had had
ample justification for deciding to save the principle of
continuation education by sacrificing some of its details
because it was wiser to lighten a ship than to let her
sink ('Highway', September 1918, 156).

THE EDUCATION ACT, 1918

On 8 August 1918, almost a year to the day since H.A.L.
Fisher had introduced the 1917 Education Bill in the House
of Commons, the 1918 Education Bill received the Royal
Assent and was placed on the statute book after having
been wisely piloted through the Commons by Fisher and his
Welsh lieutenant, Herbert Lewis. This partnership recalls
the later one of R.A. Butler and James Chuter Ede forged
during the shaping of the 1944 Education Act. It had also
been expertly guided through the Lords by the Earl of
Lytton.

In carrying the Bill, Fisher had had, at times, to bow
to pressures from certain directions and modify original
intentions but, in the majority of cases, efforts to

extend or amend proposals had been resisted. Attempts, also, to delay the 1918 Bill by overloading it had been thwarted. This fear had been expressed, for example, in the Commons on 7 May 1918, during the debate on the provision of secondary education, by Sir William Pearce (L., Tower Hamlets, Limehouse), a director of a chemical firm.

In addition to those provisions which have been mentioned, there were clauses in the Act dealing with the education of physically defective and epileptic children and those in exceptional circumstances; the power to aid research; the provision of maintenance allowances and the appointment of certain classes of teachers. There was also reference to the closing of schools, the grouping of non-provided schools of the same denominational character, the acquisition of land by a local education authority, public enquiries by the Board of Education and educational trusts.

Congratulations from many sources flooded in to the government and Board of Education. The Archbishops of Canterbury and York, as well as the National Society, expressed their gratitude for the liberal and sympathetic attitude which had been shown by the government to voluntary effort. In return, Fisher thanked the Archbishop of Canterbury for the invaluable help that had been given to him at every stage of the Bill by the Church of England and the wise and broad-minded attitude that Holland, the secretary of the National Society, had adopted throughout (Bell, 1952, 889; Burgess and Welsby, 1961, 56).

The Nonconformists were pleased that the 1918 Education Bill had become law. The National Council of the Evangelical Free Churches announced that the Bill had received its support and that this had been communicated to Lloyd George. But the Council had not abandoned its desire for reforms in the education system which it felt would remove the serious grievances of Nonconformists that still existed, particularly in rural districts. It recognized, however, that war-time was not a suitable time for raising such questions and that everything should be done to aid the government's improvements in education (PP, National Council of the Evangelical Free Churches, 1918-19).

The Roman Catholics, when they analysed the government's intentions, estimated that they had emerged with substantial improvements so far as their interests were concerned and that even in cases where they had not obtained all that they had sought, had drawn explanations and assurances from the government, which, while tending to mitigate their immediate disappointment, might also prove of value in the future ('Tablet Educational Supplement', 27 July 1918, 97).

Reflecting on the effects of the 1918 Education Act, the NUT thought that it would benefit teachers and proclaimed on 10 August 1918, 'We now see the educationist standing on a Pisgah, with more than a hope of entering into the visioned land' (PP, NUT, 1918-19). On 19 December 1918, Sir J.H. Yoxall (L., Nottingham, W.), General Secretary of the NUT, Editor of the 'Schoolmaster', and one who had taken a close interest in the progress of the 1917 and 1918 Education Bills, wrote to Fisher thanking him for the services that he had rendered to education and the teachers by carrying through both the Education Act, 1918, and the School Teachers' (Superannuation) Act, 1918, which had been passed on 21 November 1918 (PP, NUT, 1918-19).

While apprehensive about the implications of certain sections of the 1918 Education Act which could mean that all private schools would eventually come under some sort of state inspection, that inefficient schools were likely to be summarily dealt with, while even the efficient ones would be liable to attention, the Private Schools Association decided to look at the matter realistically. In order to forestall criticism, it was decided that all private schools should not only make themselves efficient but should also be especially careful about those 'outward and visible signs' which might reasonably be supposed to accompany efficiency. Suggesting the accurate keeping of attendance registers and records, the PSAI stressed, as well, that care should be taken that classrooms were well ventilated and that all books and apparatus were kept clean and properly housed ('Secondary Education', September 1918, 70).

The Labour movement still wished, however, that the planners of the 1918 Education Bill had gone further. At its conference in January 1918, the Labour Party urged amendments to Fisher's revised Bill which would make it 'a complete Charter of National Education from the Primary School to the University'. Some delegates expressed the hope that Labour MPs would fight for the 'Bradford Charter'. Similar views were uttered at the special Labour Party Conference held in July 1918 (Simon, 1965, 356). The WEA had issued its amendments to the Bill in April 1918 (WEA, April 1918, 7).

R.H. Tawney had also added his views to the dissatisfaction of the Labour movement by observing in the 'Daily News' of 14 February 1918 that the aim of education in the FBI's Memorandum on Education was 'to reflect, to defend and to perpetuate the division of mankind into master and servants' and that 'The Bourbons of industry who drafted it have learned nothing and forgotten nothing. Europe is

in ruins; and out of the sea of blood and tears the Federation of British Industries emerges jaunty and unabashed
clamouring that whatever else is shaken, the vested
interest of employers in the labour of children of four-
teen must not be disturbed by so much as eight hours a
week' (Tawney, 1964, 49-51).

Arthur Henderson, however, who was Chairman of the
Parliamentary Party 1914-17 and Party Secretary 1912-34,
on 25 May 1918, while regretting that the government's
plans fell short of Labour's own educational programme,
was one influential Labour supporter who welcomed them
because, at least, they were instalments of long overdue
reforms and a base from which further progress might continue ('The Times', 27 May 1918, 6).

Of the other lobbies which had watched so closely the
odysseys of the 1917 and 1918 Education Bills through
Parliament, the National Education Association, the
Teachers' Guild Council, the Superintendents of School
Attendance Departments for England and Wales and the
Society of Friends (Quakers) welcomed the Act. So did the
Training College Association and the British and Foreign
School Society which had been engaged for a hundred years
in the training of teachers.

Applause for the Act also came from the Froebel
Society, the Association of Teachers of Domestic Subjects
and the Association of Technical Institutions. Later,
after its foundation in 1923, The Nursery School Association of Great Britain praised the Fisher Act. The Ling
Association (now The Physical Education Association of
Great Britain and Northern Ireland) was pleased, too, by
the government's legislation but it had been concerned
that, during wartime, military drill might be introduced
in schools under the clause dealing with social and physical training. The British Science Guild was another body
which approved the government's proposals for educational
reform. It had welcomed, in particular, the plans for all
elementary and continuation school children to receive
instruction in practical subjects provided that such
teaching did not involve direct tuition for a trade
('Education', 22 February 1918).

The medical profession welcomed the improvements which
the Act made possible in the education and physical welfare (and therefore in the efficiency and happiness) of
the population. It also considered that the duties and
powers granted to the local education authorities under
the Act were of a far-reaching character ('British Medical
Journal', 7 September 1918, 259-60).

By the time of the passing of the 1918 Education Act,
such voluntary bodies as the Boys' Brigade and the Scout

Association had come to see ways in which the activities
of local education authorities could be supplemented by
those of their associations. Initially, the legislation
in the 1917 and 1918 Education Bills dealing with the provision of continuation schools, holiday camps, playing
fields and social and physical training had drawn from
them the fear that their activities might be curtailed by
such provision ('Boys' Brigade Gazette', December 1919,
57-8; 'Chief Scouts' Outlook', April and September 1918)

The Shaftesbury Society and Ragged School Union was
another group that favoured the Act. In particular, it
had supported the creation of continuation schools because
it had believed that the extension of school life through
the difficult period of adolescence would be of vast physical and moral advantage to the class of children and young
persons that the Society sought to serve.

In his War Memoirs (1933, 1079), David Lloyd George,
who had plucked his President of the Board of Education
from the groves of academe and tossed him into the hurly-
burly of political life, subsequently paid tribute to the
extreme skill that Fisher had shown in conducting the 1918
Bill through Parliament. He observed that no one since
W.E. Forster had left such an impression on the system of
education and that the President had contributed to one of
the most important chapters in educational history by
placing the 1918 Education Bill on the statute book.

The anti-collectivist movement, which at one time had
looked as if it would annihilate the government's plans
for educational reform, had, therefore, been thrust back.

THE LIGHTS COME ON AGAIN

On 8 August 1918, as the Education Bill received the Royal
Assent, Ludendorff, the German military leader, only too
conscious of the fact that Germany was starving because of
the successful blockade by the Allied Navy and that her
allies were collapsing, advised the Fatherland to seek
peace. On 11 November 1918, after threats of revolution
because the civilian population could suffer no more and
the flight of Kaiser Wilhelm from Berlin to Holland on 9
November 1918, the heavy guns fell silent, nations every-
where closed their eyes in prayers of thankfulness, the
Armistice was signed in a railway coach in Compiègne
forest and a war which had witnessed carnage and suffering
of an unparalleled kind to that date in the world and
which had involved civilian populations of many countries
on an unprecedented scale was at an end. Slowly, lights
were lit, their rays penetrated the gloom and people of

previously warring nations looked up and about them, uncertainly, in a changed world.

Chapter four

The aftermath

THE NEW ERA

In Paris, on 28 June 1919, in the Galerie des Glaces of
the Palace of Louis XIV, where the German Empire had been
proclaimed by Bismarck in 1871 following the defeat of
France in the Franco-Prussian War, a peace settlement with
Germany was signed by the Entente at the Treaty of
Versailles. Other treaties with Germany's allies followed.
The conclusion of the war, and the treaties, witnessed the
end of the Hohenzollern, Habsburg, Romanoff and Ottoman
dynasties. Small nation states like Czechoslovakia were
either created or reborn like Poland under the terms of
the Versailles Treaty. The first annual Assembly of the
League of Nations, which was formed to ensure peace for
all time, was opened on 14 December 1920 at Geneva in
Switzerland (Mowat, 1956, I).

With the coming of peace, nations struggled to repair
the devastation wrought by the First World War, and, by
tilling and irrigating waste lands, to build homes fit for
heroes to live in. Tragically, however, during the long,
critical years filled with agitation, economic collapse
and famine following the peace settlement with Germany,
countries were deprived of the invaluable services of the
millions killed and maimed in the war, many of them
possessed of the highest talents.

Demobilization commenced in Britain after the signing
of the Armistice on 11 November 1918. Later, the official
date for the termination of the war was fixed at 10 January 1920. Because it had been agreed that there would be
a return after the war to a form of government with less
rule from the centre, the controls of trade and shipping
were allowed to end in 1919, the rationing of food and
most price controls ceased by 1920 and factories and war
surplus goods were sold off. Much of the collective

mechanism, however, which had been erected during the war
in order to prosecute it more successfully was retained.
In some cases there were extensions to it such as the
creations, for example, of the Ministries of Health and
Transport in 1919.

The Lloyd George Coalition Government which was
returned at the General Election of December 1918 with an
overwhelming majority by an electorate swelled by the
extension of the franchise to women, as well as men not
previously eligible to vote, faced a difficult period.
This meant, at home, following the boom economic period of
1918 and 1919, strikes, an influenza epidemic, a critical
housing shortage, rapidly rising prices, multiplying
unemployment which by 1921 had reached over 2,000,000 of
a population of about forty-four million souls, and then
economic collapse. Abroad, the government had to contend
with disquiet in Ireland, India and Palestine (ibid.)

The result was that during 1920 there was increasing
pressure on the government from many sections of the
public to counter the increasing inflation, the heavy
burden of taxation and rates, the decline in trade and
industrial activity and the rise in unemployment, by reducing the expenditure on public services. Because of this,
on 8 December 1920, after a series of heart-searching
meetings of the Cabinet when the financial crisis was
debated, all spending departments were instructed that,
except with fresh Cabinet authority, every scheme involv-
ing expenditure which was not in operation had to remain
in abeyance. The case of the special problem of unemployment, where temporary measures could be inaugurated, was
excepted from this order (BEP, December 1920).

Austen Chamberlain, the Chancellor of the Exchequer,
when explaining the Cabinet's decision to the House of
Commons on 9 December 1920, pointed out that the worsening
economic situation was due to 'the high cost of material',
'the exceptionally heavy taxation', 'and the emergency
measures required to mitigate the hardships of unemployment'. While the need for reforms was recognized, it was
submitted, however, that the time to put extra burdens on
the rates and taxes was not appropriate. On 21 December
1920, support for the government's drastic action was contained in the Seventh Report of the Select Committee of
the House of Commons on National Expenditure.

In addition to this fierce economy drive, which
resulted in savings of £75 million, the government set up
in August 1921 a committee under the chairmanship of Sir
Eric Geddes to examine all the financial estimates for
1922/3 and advise on specific economies. The upshot was
that further economies to the value of £70 million, made

up of £18 million from education, £6 million from health
and war pensions and the rest from the armed services
were proposed in the Geddes reports on national expenditure of 14 December 1921, 28 January 1922 and 21 February
1922.

Eventually, after more deliberation, the government
agreed to cuts of £64 million in national expenditure
which Sir Robert Horne, by then Chancellor of the
Exchequer, explained to the House of Commons on 1 March
1922. These cuts included pruning the expenditure on
education to the extent of about £6 million.

SCHEMES FOR THE PROGRESSIVE DEVELOPMENT OF EDUCATION

While Great Britain struggled through the troubled years
following the cessation of the First World War, local
education authorities, guided by the days appointed for
the different provisions of the 1918 Education Act
(Appendix B), commenced to draw up and submit to the
Board of Education their schemes for the organization and
progressive development of education within their areas in
accordance with Sections 1-4 of the 1918 Act, (and subsequently Sections 11-16 of the Education Act, 1921, a
consolidating Act). In Board of Education Circular 1119
of July 1919, furthermore, not only were the authorities
advised to bear their immediate needs in mind when preparing their proposals but also developments over at
least ten years. In Circular 1175 of September 1920 they
were asked to submit estimates of their costs and numbers
of teachers required to the Board for the next four to
five years.

The records surviving of those local education authorities which did submit schemes after the passing of the
1918 Education Act show them grappling with their individual problems in their attempts to reshape the educational provision in their areas along the lines suggested
by the Board of Education (BEP, 1918-32).

Thus the Kent Education Committee, for instance, had to
deal with a situation, when considering the provision of
continuation schools, of young persons resident in Kent
who went daily to work in London. The Committee eventually agreed with the London Education Committee that
young persons residing in Kent, but working in London,
would attend day continuation schools in London and that
this arrangement would come into force when the London
continuation schools opened on 1 January 1921 or there-
abouts (ibid., May 1920, January 1921).

Some rural counties, when drawing up their schemes for

educational provision, had other problems. Thus the East
Sussex Education Committee whose area was almost entirely
agricultural, residential and scattered but also bordered
in parts by a sea-coast had to overcome the obstacle of
an absence of suitable transport. This made communication
within the authority difficult. At one time it had been
suggested that since the continuation schools in East
Sussex were bound to have a rural bias, they should come
under the jurisdiction of the Board of Agriculture but
W.N. Bruce at the Education Department opposed this suggestion (ibid., 1921).

Some local education authorities, like Lancashire, when
considering their schemes for reorganization, requested
more time from the Board in which to prepare them.
Sympathetic to the request from Lancashire that it might
submit 'interim' schemes from time to time which would
later be incorporated into a complete scheme, W.N. Bruce
was insistent that the 'interim scheme' should include an
outline of the general principles on which the final
scheme would be founded (ibid., 1920).

Finally, the London County Council was one authority
which, when drawing up a scheme of education, not only
stressed the necessity for considering the historical
background of the education authority but its place in
national life. The LCC, therefore, not only bore in mind
the needs of its locality in which there was no staple
industry but also the fact that it was the commercial
home of world markets; the centre of international finance; the capital city of a world-wide Empire and the
meeting place of nearly every race (ibid., July 1920).

THE BURNHAM COMMITTEES

Fisher, it will be recalled, had always argued that it was
necessary for successful educational development to have a
contented teaching force. To help meet this aim, in the
1918 Education Act, under Section 2, it was made the duty
of local education authorities to supply and train
teachers. Prior to this, in pursuance of the same goal,
as has already been pointed out, minimum salaries had
been prescribed for certain grades of teacher. This
intention had been carried into effect by a Minute of the
Board dated 14 January 1918. Circular 1024, explaining
the effect of the Minute, had been issued to local education authorities on 22 January 1918.

Also in June 1917, a Departmental Committee, which
reported in 1918, had been appointed to look into 'the
principles which should determine the construction of

scales of salaries for teachers in elementary schools'.
This Committee had also commented adversely on the superannuation scales of teachers. Another Report of a
Departmental Committee, in July 1918, enquired into 'the
principles which should·determine the fixing of salaries
for teachers in secondary and technical schools, schools
of art, training colleges (domestic subjects), and other
institutions for higher education, (other than university
institutions)'.

In August 1919, Fisher set up the far-reaching Standing
Joint Committee composed of twenty representatives each of
the National Union of Teachers and the local education
authorities under the chairmanship of Lord Burnham 'to
secure the orderly and progressive solution of the salary
problem in public elementary schools by agreement on a
national basis and its correlation with a solution of the
salary problem in secondary schools.' In November 1919,
this Burnham Committee produced a unanimous Report on
Standard Scales of Salaries for Teachers in Public Elementary Schools recommending provisional minimum salary
scales for teachers in elementary schools. This was presented to Parliament. The scales of salaries presented by
the Burnham Committee for adoption by all concerned
granted a minimum annual salary of £160 rising by annual
increments of £10 to £300 for two years' college-trained
certificated assistant masters and for certificated
assistant mistresses £150 - £10 - £240. The pay of headmasters, which was mainly dependent on the average attendance of pupils in their schools, ranged from Grade I £330
to Grade V £450 and headmistresses Grade I £264 to Grade
V £360. Scales of salary were also devised in the Report
for uncertificated teachers and those teaching special
subjects or in special schools.

By 1 October 1920, these scales, or higher ones, were
being used by local education authorities. In the meantime, a further report, which set out three Standard
Scales, II, III and IV, and which were designed to meet
the variations in the cost of living in different areas,
was issued on 30 September 1920. Scale I appeared on 16
December 1920 and all scales were approved by the Board
of Education in 1921. The outcome of the Burnham recommendations was that there was a marked increase in
teachers' salaries with this expenditure comprising over
50 per cent of that on elementary education. Some
critics, however, felt that the increases barely enabled
teachers to keep level in their spending with the rising
cost of living.

In May 1920, a Joint Standing Committee with twenty-six
representatives each of the local education authorities

and the teachers' unions with Lord Burnham as Chairman was
formed to look at the salaries of teachers in secondary
schools in which the local education authorities accepted
responsibility for the salary scales. In its Report on
Scales of Salaries for Teachers in Secondary Schools in
which the Local Education Authorities accept Responsibility for the Salary Scales of 1 October 1920, the Committee presented for adoption salaries for graduate assistant masters ranging from £240 - £15 - £500, with a higher
scale for those teaching in London, and for non-graduates,
£190 - £12 10s - £400, with also a London scale. Comparable figures for assistant mistresses were £225 - £12 -
£400, and £177 10s - £12 10s - £320, with London scale,
as well.

By April 1921, these scales had been adopted by local
education authorities. The Burnham Committee was not able
to formulate scales of salaries for headteachers in
secondary schools because of the different kinds of
schools and varying local conditions but a minimum com-
mencing salary was fixed at £600 for a headmaster and £500
for a headmistress. All authorities were recommended,
therefore, to formulate their own scales of salaries for
headteachers bearing in mind the status of the headteacher
and 'the size and educational scope of the school'.

On 17 December 1920, a further Standing Joint Committee
under the chairmanship of Lord Burnham comprised of
twenty-four representatives each of the local education
authorities and of different associations of teachers was
constituted 'to secure by agreement on a national basis
the orderly and progressive solution of the salary problem' of teachers in technical schools, schools of art,
junior technical schools, evening schools and day continuation schools in which the local education authorities
accepted responsibility for the salary scales. In its
Report on Scales of Salaries for Teachers in Technical
Schools, Schools of Art, Junior Technical Schools,
Evening Schools and Day Continuation Schools in which the
Local Education Authorities accept Responsibility for the
Salary Scales of 28 April 1921, the Committee submitted
that graduate assistant masters in these schools should
receive an annual salary of £240 - £15 - £500, with an
additional London scale, and graduate assistant mistresses
£225 - £15 - £400, with a London scale. Non-graduate
assistant masters should receive £190 - £12 10s - £400,
with a London scale, and non-graduate assistant mistresses
£177 10s - £12 10s - £320, with London scale.

Unable to formulate scales of salaries for full-time
principals, headmasters, headmistresses and heads of
departments and instructors because of the various kinds

of schools and differing local conditions, the Burnham
Committee recommended that all local education authorities
should formulate their own standard scales for these
appointments. It suggested that they should be comparable
to those used for similar categories of teachers in the
secondary schools in the area. The scales were to come
into operation on 1 April 1921.

In all the salary scales women teachers had been unable
to obtain the equal pay with men which they had pressed
for. This was not to come until thirty years later.

The Teachers' Superannuation Act of 21 November 1918,
which came into operation in 1919, and amended the
Elementary School Teachers (Superannuation) Acts, 1898 to
1912, was the logical complement of the improved national
salary scales. It was also an extension of the compassion
which had stirred the government to improve the salaries
of teachers. The 1918 Superannuation Act introduced a
generous non-contributory scheme based on length of service and salary earned during the last five years of service. With this went a lump sum of money estimated on a
similar basis. The general effect of the new scheme was
to pension certificated and uncertificated teachers in
elementary schools, and teachers in grant-aided places of
higher education, on terms which closely resembled those
which had previously applied to civil servants.

It is not surprising because of these detailed reforms
affecting the pay and conditions of service of teachers
that there were strong protests from them when, in 1919,
Fisher's name was linked with the Ambassador's post in
Washington and also with the India Office where he had
been helping Edwin Montague, the Secretary of State for
India.

Representations, however, to Lloyd George stressed
that it would be disastrous to move the President from the
Board of Education during the difficult period that lay
ahead and the Prime Minister paid attention to these
pleas. As a result, Fisher did not leave the Board until
the Lloyd George administration fell in November 1922,
although he assumed extra duties when normal government
was resumed after the hostilities.

SECONDARY EDUCATION FOR ALL

Another development in education after the First World
War related to the provision of secondary education for
the school population, when Fisher continued the interest
that he had shown in this area when formulating the 1918
Education Act. In October 1919, he directed, in this

connection, a Departmental Committee, under the chairmanship of E. Hilton Young, a lawyer, and Liberal MP for
Norwich, 'to inquire into the working of the existing
arrangements (a) for the award by local education authorities of scholarships tenable at secondary schools or
institutions of higher education other than universities
or institutions for the training of teachers', and '(b)
for the provision of free places in secondary schools
under the regulations of the Board of Education.'

One observation of the Hilton Young Committee in its
Report on Scholarships and Free Places of 1920 was that
'weak places in the present free place and scholarship
system' had been revealed, although tribute was paid to
the new spirit created by the 1918 Education Act. The
Committee recognized that under Section 1 of the Fisher
Act the secondary school door had been pushed open wider
for the school population because the local education
authorities, when preparing their schemes, had to show the
mode in which they were providing an education 'for all
persons capable of profiting thereby'. A revolution had
been brought about, and a new order created, under Section
4 (4) of the 1918 Act, the Committee submitted because it
stipulated that in the schemes of the local education
authorities 'adequate provision shall be made in order to
secure that children and young persons shall not be
debarred from receiving the benefits of any form of
education by which they are capable of profiting through
inability to pay fees.'

The President had requested that the Committee in its
Report recommend ways in which the existing arrangements
for the provision of secondary education could be improved
so as to make 'facilities for higher education more
generally accessible and advantageous to all classes of
the population, regard being had (inter alia) to the
migration of pupils from one school or area to another'.

Among the Committee's twenty-three recommendations in
response to Fisher's request was the desire that the
financial responsibility for the provision of free places
should be transferred from the schools to the local education authorities with each school being required to
reserve an approved minimum number of vacancies; that the
percentage of free places should be raised from 25 to 40
for each area generally, and normally for each school, and
that the number of secondary schools should be increased
so as to provide at least 20 school places for each 1,000
pupils of the school population. But there could be different kinds of secondary education.

While agreement was also reached that 11 was the most
suitable age at which a child could be transferred from an

elementary to a secondary school because, for the
majority of children, it indicated a certain stage in
their development, there was disagreement among the committee as to how the selection could be made. A formal
test which would assess 'capacity and promise rather than
attainment' was recommended by the majority.

Although the Committee recommended 'as a prospective
policy' the 'discontinuance of all fees in secondary
schools', it submitted that this should 'be carried out as
soon as the conditions of national finance allow'. The
amount of money received in fees for pupils in grant-
earning secondary schools was not large, about £2 million,
based on the estimate for £1,100,245 for 1912-13 (the last
available figure), but it was still felt that such a sum
could not be spared to relieve the financial burden of fee-
paying parents. Instead, public money should be used to
aid cleverer children and develop the much-needed alternative forms of post-elementary education.

R.H. Tawney, in his influential book 'Secondary Education for All, A Policy for Labour', which he edited for
the Education Advisory Committee of the Labour Party in
April 1922, used figures mentioned in the Report on
Scholarships and Free Places.

THE EFFECT OF THE ECONOMIC CRISIS ON EDUCATIONAL DEVELOP-
MENT

The cumulative effect of the economy cuts in education
following the Cabinet Resolution on Expenditure of 8
December 1920 and increasing pressure from business and
commercial interests, Anti-Waste campaigners, members of
all political parties and different sections of the public
unenthusiastic for educational reform (BEP, 1920-1), as
well as those disturbed by events in Bolshevik Russia, was
that by the time of the fall of the Lloyd George Coalition
in November 1922 educational development in all directions
had been brought virtually to a standstill. The pension
scheme for teachers, and their salaries, had been also
affected. The early guidelines to the local education
authorities as to how the cuts were to be implemented -
after much discussion between a defensive Board of Education and a rapacious Exchequer (BEP, 1920) - were communicated in the Board's Circulars of 1185 of 17 December 1920,
(in particular) 1190 of 11 January 1921, 1225 of 18 August
1921 and 1228 of 23 August 1921.

In spite of the drastic action which had arrested
educational expenditure and had dealt severe blows at the
implementation of the 1918 Education Act, the Geddes

Committee, in its First Interim Report on National Expenditure of 14 December 1921 argued that because the cost of each elementary and secondary school pupil had risen enormously since 1918 the net expenditure on education still far exceeded that which the nation could afford in difficult times. The result had been that the extra costs had been increasingly transferred from the local ratepayer to the taxpayer. An indication of the enlarged expenditure on education was that the Board of Education's Vote had grown from £19 million in 1918/19 to £50 million. But the value of money had declined substantially since 1918.

To bring about a saving to the taxpayer, the Geddes Committee recommended that children should not enter state-aided schools until they had reached the age of 6 and that the cost of teaching children in the schools should be reduced by the local education authorities. This could be brought about in elementary education by closing small schools, revising the standards of staffing by placing more pupils under the care of one teacher and by paying teachers less money.

Economies in higher education, it was suggested, could be made by reducing expenditure on secondary education; technical education of various kinds; the training of teachers who would subsequently teach in elementary schools and on the maintenance allowances granted by local authorities to pupils at secondary schools. In this area, the Geddes Committee maintained that the grants for secondary education were providing state-aided, or free education, for a class of people who could afford to pay an increased proportion, or even the full cost, of the education of their children. Children who were not mentally capable of benefiting from a secondary education were also receiving financial aid. The Geddes Committee accordingly recommended that higher education should be confined to those pupils whose mental calibre justified it and whose parents could not afford to pay for it. The expenditure on supplying scholarships to the universities should also be reduced.

The Superannuation scheme of teachers also came under scrutiny by the Geddes Committee in its Report because it noticed with concern that the cost of this scheme was accelerating and that it might ultimately amount to £12 million per annum. It was therefore not only recommended that the teachers should contribute 5 per cent of their salaries to their pension funds in order to reduce the burden on the Exchequer but that the whole question of teachers' superannuation should be investigated before 'the growth of vested interests makes it incapable of modification'.

A yield of £16,100,000 to the Exchequer could be obtained, the Geddes Committee suggested, by reducing the estimates for the Board of Education for the year 1922/3 from £50,600,000 to £34,500,000. This would be raised to £18 million with the automatic reductions in Scotland. It was recommended, too, that whatever proportion of the reduced sum was allocated to the local education authorities it should be allotted in such a way by the Board of Education that the percentage grant system was superseded.

Eventually there was some relief expressed in the educational world when, on 27 April 1922, after months of intense activity (during which Fisher contemplated resignation but stayed on to resist the Geddes proposals) the debates on the Board of Education's estimates for the subsequent financial year in Parliament revealed that cuts in educational expenditure would not be as severe as had been expected. The projected estimate of £50,600,000 was to be reduced by £5,700,000 to £44,900,000. Even so this meant a cut of nearly 20 per cent in the special services' estimate which dealt with the school medical services, defective children, evening play centres and nursery schools. At a time of rising unemployment the curtailment of the grant for school meals to £300,000 from £1,030,000 aroused protests. Savings were also to be brought about by supporting such Geddes recommendations as increasing the size of classes in elementary schools thus reducing the number of teachers over a period of three years by between 4,700 and 6,000. Heads of schools with less than 250 pupils were also required to teach a class. But the raising of the age of entry to school from 5 to 6 had not been accepted.

The government, however, made the serious decision to follow the Geddes recommendations to reduce educational expenditure by making teachers contribute 5 per cent of their salaries towards their superannuation fund. But the School Teachers (Superannuation) Bill introduced in the Commons on 9 May 1922 was eventually defeated during its Second Reading on 16 May. One result was that the government was forced to set up a small Select Committee of Enquiry of nine MPs to see whether Fisher, by asking the teachers to contribute towards their pensions had broken an undertaking by the government, given, or implied, that the provisions of the Teachers' Superannuation Act, 1918, should not be amended while the Burnham salary scales remained in existence. The Committee had to decide, too, whether the teachers had accepted the scales because they considered that they would eventually receive pensions on a non-contributory basis.

The Select Committee set up to investigate the matter subsequently decided by a narrow margin that no guarantee, either expressed or inferred, had been given by the government, or Parliament, that the proposals of the 1918 Teachers (Superannuation) Act should not be altered while the present salary scales remained in force.

Fisher subsequently pointed out after the Second Reading of the Superannuation Bill had been finally carried in the Commons on 3 July 1922, and, with minor amendments, had become law, that it had been decided, after a struggle, that the savings of £2 million brought about by asking the teachers to contribute to their pension fund had been preferable to making the size of classes much larger, say 60-70 pupils in continuation schools (Tropp, 1957, 219f).

Later in the year, agreement was reached with the teachers' unions about a voluntary 5 per cent cut in teachers' salaries. This commenced from 1 April 1923 (ibid., 220).

In August 1922, further draft regulations for secondary schools, which placed additional control on the number of free places in secondary schools and which threatened a further increase in fees were issued to the local authorities by the Board.

While these economies were being made, disapproval continued to be expressed by all sections of the educational world, including Lord Burnham, at the increasing control of the central authority, by means of economic cuts, over educational policy and expenditure. This meant the negation of reforms passed by Parliament. The percentage grant system had not been replaced.

CONTINUATION SCHOOLS

A conspicuous target of the government's economy measures in education was the provision of compulsory day continuation schools because the Cabinet's Finance Committee estimated that their establishment would prove too expensive. These schools had been carefully planned by the Board of Education through such Circulars as 1096 (1918), 1102 (1919), 1115 (1919), and 1118 (1919), together with advice about recruitment for the schools. Many local education authorities had planned day continuation schools under Section 10 of the Education Act, 1918, and later Section 75 of the Education Act, 1921 (MEP, 1919-47).

Fisher, in a letter dated 7 December 1920 from Geneva where he was one of the three British delegates to the League of Nations Assembly, denied this. In his letter to Sir M.P.A. Hankey (Stephen Roskill's 'Man of Secrets'),

Secretary to the Cabinet, he pointed out that the extra
expenditure on education in the succeeding years would be
mainly due to the increased salaries of teachers and not,
principally, to the carrying out of the provisions for
continuation education (CP 2346, December 1920).

Moreover, in a note to the Chancellor of the Exchequer
of 16 December 1920, Fisher attempted to gauge the charges
which were likely to fall on the Vote of the Board of
Education in the near future when providing continuation
education. This was later circulated to all members of
the Finance Committee together with an accompanying Memorandum by Austen Chamberlain 'Expenditure on Education'
dated 21 December 1920. In his note, Fisher submitted
that the cost falling on the Board's Vote was estimated
at (CP 2344, 1920):

1921-2	£300,000
1922-3	£600,000 to £700,000
1923-4 and thereafter until 1928	£750,000 to £900,000

This amount was to be shared equally between rates and
grant. This expenditure, moreover, was based on the sup-
position that the seven areas which had arranged appointed
days would proceed to carry out their schemes for introducing this form of education and that no more appointed
days would be given to other areas.

The seven areas able to suggest appointed days for the
opening of continuation schools during this critical
period, bearing in mind, as requested by the Board, that
they would have adequate buildings and teachers with which
a start could be made, were Stratford-on-Avon (Warwickshire) (12 April 1920); Rugby UD (13 April 1920); Birmingham CB (23 August 1920); Swindon Borough (20 September
1920); Southend-on-Sea CB (2 November 1920); Kent (for
those young people employed in London) (11 November 1920);
Warwickshire (for those employed in Rugby UD (10 January
1922). The estimated numbers of young people attending
the schools were as in Table 1 (page 74).

In the event Southend soon discontinued its prepara-
tions for opening schools and Kent made no arrangement for
enforcing the attendance of young persons residing in Kent
but working in London. Other authorities, like Birmingham and London, began to approach the Board of Education
with requests to be released from the statutory obligation
to provide day continuation schools. Eventually the
Cabinet agreed (with Fisher disagreeing, however) that the
necessary legislation should be passed which would relieve
those authorities which were under statutory obligation to
provide day continuation schools for children in their
areas from doing so (BEP 1924; CP 27/22(5), 1922; HAC
112(1)(a), 1922).

TABLE 1

LEAS with appointed days	Estimated number of persons aged 14-16 years	Average number that might be required throughout the year to attend continuation schools if available		
		1921-2	1922-3	1923-4
London	120,000	52,500	108,750	120,000
Stratford	400	225	387	400
Rugby	800	450	775	800
Birmingham	30,000	13,125	27,188	30,000
West Ham	12,000	5,250	10,875	12,000
Swindon	1,840	805	1,667	1,840
Southend	2,496	1,092	2,262	2,496
	167,536	73,447	151,904	167,536

Source: ibid.

The decision that no more appointed days for providing continuation education should be agreed was communicated to the local education authorities on 11 January 1921 by Circular 1190. But by this time no local education authority, because of the mounting concern about the economy, was seriously asking for an appointed day. Middlesex, which was prepared to make young persons resident in Middlesex and working in London subject to the same obligation as applied to young persons resident in London, was the exception. The continuation school at Rugby was one that continued to remain open because Rugby was the only local authority that implemented the relevant clauses of the 1918 Education Act. It finally closed in 1969.

At the same time as some authorities were struggling to bring into being compulsory day continuation schools, in Manchester, Bolton, Bristol, Eastbourne, Reading and in certain places in Lancashire, Cheshire, Yorkshire (W. Riding) and Warwickshire, new day continuation schools were opened on the basis of the co-operation between local education authorities and employers. These were those employers who were prepared either to make attendance at school a condition of employment or to permit time off for attendance. Some of these schools were conducted on the premises of the employers. But in the course of time it

became plain that many local education authorities were
not prepared to spend money on such schools and they
became Works Schools. Manchester and Bristol, for
example, were authorities which, from the beginning, had
undertaken considerable financial and educational responsibilities for the work in the voluntary schools (BEP,
1924).

When the economy cuts were introduced with the dis-
appearance of the possibility of compulsory attendance
for young people at day continuation schools, many employers also became lukewarm about carrying on the voluntary
continuation schools. Foremen in industrial firms who had
not taken kindly to a system that disturbed the ordinary
routine of juvenile employment saw a way of releasing
themselves from the burdens created by the voluntary
system. The trade depression, furthermore, made employers
less able and less willing to meet whatever extra expense
might have fallen upon them through the continuation
school experiment. Parents of the young people involved,
moreover, did not always view favourably the loss of working time and subsequent forfeiture of wages. The result
was that for these, and other reasons, many voluntary
schools also closed in the early 1920s (ibid., 1924).

At first, it must be noted, a high percentage of those
young people who were under an obligation to enrol at a
continuation school did so, with subsequent regular
attendance. Gradually a serious decline in enrolment and
regularity of attendance set in. By the time of the
school year ending 31 July 1923, Charles Trevelyan,
President of the Board of Education, explained to the
Commons on 21 March 1924 that about 12,600 boys and
10,800 girls were enrolled in schools or classes of the
day continuation school type (Hansard, 21 March 1924,
808).

END OF AN ERA

The few years since the termination of the war had indeed
been traumatic ones. The attempts to create a brave new
world from the débris of the old had received many set-
backs. Determined rearguard actions had, however, preserved the majority of the educational reforms of the 1918
Education Act. But the years were not entirely ones of
gloom and depression. They were laced with gaiety. For
some they were even glittering years full of dancing and
laughter. For an increasing number housing conditions
improved. The use also of the gramophone and wireless,
for example, enriched many lives and widened horizons.

The moment when Fisher relinquished his seals of office to King George V at Buckingham Palace after the fall of the Lloyd George Coalition in October 1922 was a melancholy one for him. He remained as a backbencher for a period and then, in 1926, became Warden of New College, Oxford, in succession to the famous Dr Spooner. In 1940, he was killed in an accident on the Embankment, London.

Lloyd George never again held high political office. Neither was the Liberal Party ever returned to power.

Chapter five

An assessment of the Education Act, 1918

How does one evaluate an Education Act? What makes one
Act in educational history seem more important to some
people than another? What are the criteria that can be
used? Is it possible to make a final judgment? These
are not easy questions to answer and it is obvious that
one should always be prepared to look at the long term
influences of an Act as well as the short term; to realize
that an Education Act cannot always be immediately and
completely successful and that only a few of its provisions might be implemented.

It would seem, however, bearing all this in mind, that
behind the judgments which make educationists almost universally decide that the 1870, 1902 and 1944 Education
Acts were significant was the fact that they all altered
the structure of the educational system in some way, as
well as carrying out other reforms, although in some
cases of a limited nature. Thus under the 1870 Education
Act, school boards were brought into being and subsequently the board schools. Under the 1902 Act the school
boards were replaced by the local education authorities
with the Dual System being adjusted into provided and non-
provided schools. Under the 1944 Education Act, the
number of the local education authorities was not only
curtailed and their composition simplified but the Dual
System was modified yet again with the formation of different categories of voluntary schools such as 'controlled', 'aided', and 'special agreement'.

Under the 1918 Education Act the structure of the
educational system was not markedly altered. This meant
that the 317 local education authorities were still responsible for education in their different areas.

In order to establish 'a national system of public
education available for all persons capable of profiting
thereby', the local education authorities had, however,

under Section 1 of the 1918 Education Act, to prepare a
series of schemes showing how they planned to develop
education in their areas. These were to be submitted to
the Board of Education for approval. But a feature of the
1918 Act was the intention to form a close working
partnership between the authorities and the Board of Education by placing more responsibility for the work of
education on the local authorities. The Board of Education, when schemes were submitted to them, was to act,
therefore, more as an advisory body. It was to see, however, that suitable schemes were submitted and that,
later, they were carried out.

Many new powers and duties were also conferred on the
local education authorities of all grades in an attempt to
form a closer partnership between the Board of Education
and the local authorities; to eliminate the variety of
authorities and to enable one authority in an area to have
its own definite responsibility. Thus, under Section 6 of
the 1918 Education Act, councils were able to co-operate
or combine with other councils in order to carry out more
successfully their duties. Under this arrangement they
could also delegate any of their powers and duties to
joint committees of councils, or joint bodies of managers.
They could not delegate the raising of a rate or the
borrowing of money.

Two or more councils, with the approval of the Board of
Education, under Section 6 of the 1918 Act, could also
band in federations to deal with matters of common
interest which could be more conveniently dealt with in
larger areas. These interests included the training of
teachers; higher education; the supply of scholarships
and provision for advanced technical and research work.
The councils could also delegate the whole of their powers
to the federations, except, again, that of raising a rate
or borrowing money.

The powers of the local education authorities were also
extended under the Act when dealing with the church
schools. Thus, in non-provided schools, teachers of practical subjects, pupil teachers, student teachers and all
teachers of secular subjects not attached to the staff of
any particular elementary school, had to be appointed,
under Section 29, by the local education authority.
Again, managers of confessional schools could not close a
school without giving eighteen months' notice to the local
authority. Should the managers fail to carry on the
school during the prescribed period the authority could,
under Section 30 of the Act, carry it on in the school
premises as a provided school.

A local education authority might, with the approval

of the Board of Education, give orders under Section 31 of
the 1918 Act for the grouping of voluntary schools of the
same denomination and for the distribution of the children
in such schools according to age, sex or attainment.

Although these adjustments to the relationship between
the local education authorities and the voluntary schools
were made in the 1918 Education Act to meet the needs of
changing times and the views expressed during the debates
on the 1918 Education Bill, the Dual System, as such, was
not drastically amended in the Act. Wisely, the religious
issue was left alone because it was too soon after the
controversies caused by the passing of the 1902 Education
Act.

The later, unsuccessful, attempt by Fisher in 1919 and
1920 to deal with the problem, when he suggested that
local education authorities should take over complete control of all non-provided schools with, in return, 'facilities' in the schools for denominational instruction at
parents' requests, showed that the time was still not
suitable. On this occasion, the proposals for a system of
contracting out were rejected by the churches with the
teachers' unions being deeply suspicious that the plan
would mean religious tests for teachers. The Education
Act (1921) Amendment Bill introduced by T. Davies (L.,
Gloucester, Cirencester and Tewkesbury), on 1 November
1921 in the House of Commons, based on the Fisher proposals, was abandoned (Cruikshank, 1963, 115-20). The
deteriorating economic situation in late 1920 also abet-
ted in bringing official negotiations to a stop. Supporters of reform had, therefore, not found it possible to
transfer to another climate the relatively uncomplicated
process of the Scottish solution contained in the Education (Scotland) Act of 1918 whereby tests for teachers
ensured that children could receive denominational teaching in the schools.

Fisher continued to hold the view 'that almost any form
of settlement, which provided safeguards against the
imposition of religious tests on teachers, and against the
enforcement of religious teaching unpalatable to the
parents of the child, would be preferable to the continu-
ance of the present arrangement ...' (Fisher, 1923b, 447).
But he held very strongly that the religious concordat
had to come from the churches themselves and that perhaps
the churches of the Protestant faith at least could reach
some agreement.

The system of finance was also simplified and improved
with the introduction of the percentage grant system under
Section 44 of the 1918 Education Act. This meant that the
Board of Education had full power to pay grants to a local

education authority in respect of any expenditure which the authority might lawfully incur. This would normally take the form of not less than half the expenditure of a local education authority on elementary or higher education provided that the regulations laid down by the Board of Education were complied with. If the grant as calculated proved to be less than one half of the total net expenditure a deficiency grant was paid to make it up to one half. In calculating the deficiency grant any grants paid by any other government department would be taken into account. If an authority failed in its duties, or if the conditions of grant as laid down by the Board of Education were not complied with, a deduction might be made from the percentage grant, or the deficiency grant reduced.

In the years that followed, this arrangement survived the recommendations of the Geddes Committee for its removal but the 50 per cent minimum grant was withdrawn as a result of the 1931 crisis following the advice of the May Committee's Report on National Expenditure, 1931. The percentage grant system was not replaced until the general grant system was introduced in 1959.

Under Section 2 of the Fisher Act attention was directed to the supply and training of teachers because it was realized that an adequate teaching force was essential for educational reform. This was made the responsibility of the local education authorities. In 1923, 7,678 students completed various courses of training for work in elementary schools the Report of the Board of Education Departmental Committee on the Training of Teachers for Public Elementary Schools stated in 1925.

The solicitude shown for the teachers with the increase of salary scales and improved pension rights was much appreciated by them and a notable step forward. It had been realized by the government that the increase of salaries and the extension of superannuation benefits would mean less money for other reforms. But Fisher wished all 'friends of education' to 'strenuously resist the view that a slave-ration of knowledge administered by mechanical drudges is adequate to the needs of one of the most gifted populations in the world' (Fisher, 1923b, 447).

Progress in this direction could continue, Fisher felt, by the Board of Education announcing that the grant to local education authorities would be withheld if the teachers were paid too low a salary. In this way the teachers' pay would be adequate and certain, teachers' strikes could be avoided, and the atmosphere of salary discussions improved.

In addition, under Section 8 of the 1918 Education Act, in order to keep a child within the beneficial influence of an educational institution, boys and girls had to attend school between the ages of 5 and 14 with no exemptions. This also meant that the half-time system of employment of children, which had imposed such a crippling strain on their strength, was finally abolished under the Act. Local education authorities were able to raise the leaving age to 15 if they so desired and to 16 or later, if suitable courses of instruction were provided. Under Section 52 (3) of the Act, however, these arrangements could not take place before the termination of the war.

On 16 May 1922, under Section 52 (3) of the Fisher Act, the Board made an order which meant that from 1 July 1922 exemptions from school before the end of the term during which a child reached the age of 14 could not be granted (RBE, 1921-2, 2).

Because of the economic situation, and also due to the Treasury request for local education authorities not to embark on any new ventures, governments during the early 1920s were reluctant to approve by-laws raising the leaving age to 15. In 1923, for instance, Stanley Baldwin wrote to E.F.L. Wood, President of the Board of Education, stating that he would 'be most apprehensive about relaxing in any degree the Government's present policy with regard to raising the school age' (BEP, 1923).

A by-law could also be made by a local education authority, under Section 8 of the 1918 Act, with the approval of the Board of Education, and bearing in mind the number of nursery schools in an area, to raise the age of entry to school to 6.

Local education authorities, under Section 19 of the 1918 Education Act, were encouraged to supply the new nursery school for children over 2 or under 5, or a later age if agreed by the Board. Fees in elementary schools were abolished under Section 26 of the Act.

Attention was directed to the curriculum in elementary education when, under Section 2, it was made the duty of the authorities to provide advanced work either in the elementary schools or in selective or non-selective central schools. There had been those who had argued that many children had not been extended intellectually during their final years in the elementary school.

The onus was also placed on local authorities under Section 2 of the Act to extend the curriculum by supplying more practical instruction in elementary schools. This practical instruction was defined, under Section 48 of the Act, as cookery, laundrywork, housewifery, dairywork, handicrafts and gardening. Previously ranking as special

subjects, and receiving special grants, this practice had
implied that they were outside the normal curriculum and
had encouraged dilatory authorities to regard them as
luxuries or 'frills'.

Other practical subjects could be added by the Board of
Education. By 1919-20, the Board was able to announce
that all local education authorities, with the exception
of two, had taken action in the matter (RBE, 1919-20, 24).
The importance of extending the conception of practical
instruction, especially of older pupils, was also contained in the Board's Circular 1161 of May 1920.

There was a steady increase, too, following the lead
given in the Fisher Act, in the numbers of junior technical schools. In 1917-18, there had been 61. This had
increased to 78 by 1919-20 and to 86 in 1922-3 with 10,413
boys and 1,793 girls (Spens Report, 1938, passim). No
figures are available for the number of central schools.

In order that the children would be in a suitable
physical condition to benefit from the improved arrangements and opportunities in the schools, the duty of a
local authority to provide medical inspection, with the
power to provide treatment, was extended, under Section 18
of the 1918 Act, to all children in all schools. This
meant that a child had to be medically examined immediately before entering school, or at the time of admission,
or as soon after as could be arranged. The Board of Education was to direct when further inspections were to be
made.

When attending to the health and physical condition of
the children, local education authorities were encouraged
to assist any voluntary agencies in this work. The cost,
however, of medical treatment for a child could be
charged to the parent if the authority so decided. The
authority when providing treatment also had to consider
how far the services of private medical practitioners
could be utilized but a general domiciliary service was
forbidden under Section 25 of the 1918 Act.

By 1923, the number of school clinics in England and
Wales had risen from 480 to 971 which Fisher considered a
profitable expenditure of public money (Fisher, 1923a,
515). Provision was also made under Section 20 of the
Act, for physically defective and epileptic children.
Boarding and lodging accommodation was made available
under Section 21 for children in exceptional circumstances.

The excessive out-of-school labour of children was curtailed under Section 13 of the Fisher Act when the employment of children under 12 was prohibited and strict limi-
tations were placed upon the hours that pupils worked

between the ages of 12 and 16. The employment of a child
in a factory, workshop, mine or quarry was forbidden
entirely under Section 14 of the 1918 Act in the case of a
child who was not lawfully employed at the time of the
appointed day for the implementation of Section 14.
Like compulsory attendance at school, this meant that from
1 July 1922 the prohibition extended to the end of the
term during which a child attained the age of 14. For
those blind, deaf, defective or epileptic children attending special schools, the prohibition contained in Section
14 of the 1918 Act extended to the age of 16 or the end of
the term in which that age was attained (RBE, 1921-2, 3).

Arrangement was made, too, under Section 17, for the
social and physical training of children, whereby, in
addition to the instruction provided in schools, authorities could also provide holiday or school camps, physical
training centres, playing fields, school baths and school
swimming baths for young persons attending any of the educational institutions. This also applied to young people
over 18. It is therefore not surprising, because of these
reforms, that the Fisher Act was known for a long time as
'The Children's Charter'.

The government had been perturbed by the fact that even
when the school-leaving age of children had been raised,
and large sums of money had been spent on the education of
children up to this time, the majority of children left
school never to return to the beneficial influence of an
educational institution so that much of what they had
gained at school was lost.

To remedy this situation, the government devised under
Sections 10, 11 and 12 of the 1918 Education Act the free
day continuation school which meant that seven years from
the appointed day attendance at continuation schools for
320 hours a year would become compulsory for young persons
between the ages of 16 and 18 subject to certain exceptions. Meanwhile, young persons up to the age of 16 had,
with exceptions, from an appointed day, to attend a continuation school for 320 hours in each year unless this
was reduced by the authority to 280.

The government had not expected that its continuation
school proposals would be put into immediate operation
because the cost, for example, by 1923, of introducing a
complete system of day continuation schools for young
people aged 14-18 years had doubled from the original
£10 million. The large increase in teachers' salaries
and pension rights which Fisher calculated as about equal
to twice the cost of a complete system of continuation
schools also meant that less money was available for
other reforms. Because of this, it was accepted that the
full development of day continuation schools would be the

last of the major educational reforms in the 1918 Education Act to be accomplished. In the meantime, in spite of
the financial crisis, it was hoped that much pioneer work
would be carried out in part-time voluntary continuation
schools (Fisher, 1923b, 444).

In the Fisher Act, an attempt was made to provide more
opportunities of secondary education for the school population, a factor which is often overlooked. The confining
of the rate for higher education to 2d, as has been noted,
had curbed the activities of authorities that had wished
to provide more secondary education for children. The
abolition of the financial limit under Section 44 of the
Fisher Act gave them more freedom of action in this
direction.

Under Section 1 of the Act, local education authorities, when submitting their schemes to the Board of Education for the 'progressive development and comprehensive
organization of education' in their areas, were asked to
bear in mind the capabilities of all children, and, under
Section 2, consider 'the preparation of children for further education in schools other than elementary, and their
transference at suitable ages to such schools'. Under
Clause 4, moreover, the chances of pupils to claim maintenance allowances were extended to enable them to receive
an education from which they were capable of benefiting.

Well aware of the pressures from different quarters to
provide more full-time education in secondary schools for
children, the government had considered that many poor
families could not afford to allow their children to stay
on at school until they were 16 or more. It was therefore
felt that the solution was to provide an ample supply of
free places in secondary schools, varied according to
industrial and social conditions, for those children of
parents who could not pay the fees; who wanted their
children to receive a secondary education and whose children were capable of receiving it. This was in addition to
providing continuation schools. Under this arrangement,
it was also felt that the valuable revenue provided by
school fees would not be lost. It was submitted by Fisher
that when the finance of the country was on a sounder
footing the nation might then afford free secondary education for all children (ibid., 519).

A highly selective school system geared to preparing an
élite industrial class governed by the 'survival of the
fittest' theory of social Darwinism, as had been suggested, for instance, by F.W. McConnell in 1917, was not
envisaged by Fisher, although he was sympathetic to the
needs of industry. Rather he had in mind a system which
considered the intellectual capabilities of all boys and
girls.

Meanwhile Fisher hoped that the curricula and teaching methods in the secondary schools would be improved 'without any additional outlay of public money' with close attention being paid to the suggestions of the committees which had reported on the teaching of English, classics, modern languages and science. Regard should also be directed to the differences in teaching boys and girls where evidence suggested that the education of girls suffered from being modelled too closely on that of boys (ibid., 445).

By 1923, under the stimulus given by the 1918 Education Act, the number of pupils in secondary schools on the grant list had increased from 216,765 pupils in 943 schools in 1917 to 327,601 pupils in 1,137 schools in 1923-4 (RBE, 1923-4, 67).

The number of free places in these secondary (grammar) schools had also increased after the passing of the 1918 Education Act. In 1915 the number of free places had been 65,799, or 33.1 per cent of the total number. By October 1922, this number had risen to 113,405, or 34.2 per cent (ibid.).

At the same time there were more, and more highly paid teachers, the scholars were more competently taught and their school life had been prolonged. The examination system had also been simplified and improved with the introduction in 1917 of the School and Higher Certificate Examinations to replace the many examinations formulated since the Oxford and Cambridge Local Examinations in 1858 (Beloe Report, 1960, 5). It was here rather than anywhere else that Fisher considered that the advance in education had been the most impressive. This he found the more gratifying because state-aided secondary education was comparatively new in England.

This work of providing a ladder from the elementary school to the university was continued in 1920 when 200 state scholarships were made available by the Board of Education, in co-operation with the local education authorities, for the first time, for young men and women. The scholarships included a maintenance allowance of up to £80 and the payment of tuition fees (ME, 1950, 100).

Fisher was later to draw attention to the fact that during his Presidency the highway from the school to the university had been broadened; that the state had never been so liberal with scholarships, maintenance allowances and free places. He also put forward the controversial point of view that it was unlikely an able child, no matter how poor his home, could fail to obtain the kind of education he needed, a grievance that had been aired for some time (Fisher, 1923b, 521).

By 1923, 26,500 ex-service students had received a university, or other higher education, with the help of state
grants.   In 1918, £8 million had been allocated by the
government for this purpose (ME, 1950, 101; Fisher, 1940,
114).   Some of these ex-service men trained from 1919-23
as elementary school teachers either in the normal training colleges or in the temporary Ministry of Labour
Colleges established in collaboration with the Board of
Education.   By June 1923, the last of the 1,013 men had
been examined and by October 1923 nearly all had found
teaching posts (RBE, 1922-3, 128).

The universities experienced a shortage of financial
resources after the First World War when they wanted to
meet the increased demand for a university education, as
well as planning new courses for the post-war era.   But
they had no wish to fall under the complete control of the
Board of Education.   While there was no provision in the
1918 Education Act directly affecting the universities
because they were independent, autonomous bodies function-
ing outside the jurisdiction of the Board of Education,
guarding closely their academic freedom to provide their
own courses and by carrying out fundamental research to
advance knowledge, Fisher helped in 1919 to establish the
University Grants Committee which advised the Exchequer
about the allocation of grants to the universities.   Their
independence was thus preserved although money was chan-
nelled to them.

In 1919, there appeared the influential Final Report of
the Adult Education Committee on Adult Education which
recommended, inter alia, that active participation in
adult education by the universities should be a normal and
necessary part of their function.

In addition to improving the education given in the
state system of education, an attempt was made under the
1918 Education Act to enhance the education offered by
private schools and other schools not receiving grants
from the Board of Education.   For the first time these
schools were recognized as falling within the sphere of
state responsibility and, because of this, under Section
28 of the 1918 Act, information about such schools had to
be forwarded to the Board of Education within three months
of the appointed day.   If they so desired, such schools
could also avail themselves of the medical inspection and
treatment provided by the local education authority of the
area.   They could also take advantage, under Section 27,
of a free inspection and report by the Board of Education
to the governing body or headmaster.   As part of accepting
the proposals of the Act, Harrow and Rugby, for example,
between 1919 and 1921, were two of the nine schools

recognized by the Board following inspection (Bamford, 1967, X; Graves, 1940, 187).

On 3 April 1919, Fisher was unable to agree to an offer from representatives of the Headmasters' Conference for some public schools to mix the social classes in their schools by accepting a certain number of poor pupils from the elementary schools thereby qualifying for state financial aid. Some of the schools were in financial difficulties during the post-war period owing to a fall in numbers, the need to pay teachers at the new rates of pay and to meet the pension requirements of the Teachers' Superannuation Act of 1918.

While appreciating the soundness of the offer which Fisher considered augured well for the future of education, he thought that the financial implications were too much for the time. It was also considered too controversial an issue. Nor was there any demand, it was felt, from elementary school children for places in public schools. Fisher held that schools in the independent sector of education might render a useful service by educating pupils from other schools at the relatively late age of 15 or over. The offer was not taken up (Bamford, 1967, 287-8).

Parents were also encouraged to express their views about educational development under the terms of the 1918 Education Act. When submitting their schemes under Section 1 for the progressive organization of education in their areas, for example, local education authorities were asked to consider any representations made to them by parents about the schemes. Under Section 8 of the Act, any ten parents of children attending elementary schools could request a public enquiry if a local education authority contemplated raising the age of entry to school from 5 to 6 years. It was subsequently hoped that, with the parents taking a closer interest in educational provision, they would become more familiar with the facilities available for their children, such as those dealing with scholarship places and financial assistance, and would accordingly make use of them.

In addition to producing a successful solution to contemporary problems, the shapers of the Fisher Act built a secure jumping-off ground for later thought and legislation. The Hadow Committee, in its Report on the Education of the Adolescent, 1926, when acknowledging its debt to the 1918 Act, recognized 'that in education, as in other departments of social policy, it is not possible to proceed per saltum, that no generation ever has a clean sheet on which to write', and that 'each generation must build with materials inherited from the past on pain of not

building at all ...' (Hadow Report, 77).   In the Butler
Education Act of 1944, many of the recommendations of the
Fisher Education Act were extended to meet the needs of
changing times.

The seeds of future reform were sown during the years
of ordeal of the First World War in the 1918 Education
Act; even such proposals as the establishment of nursery
and continuation schools, which did not develop in the way
that had been hoped, were continually referred to in later
years and legislated for once again in 1944.   Unfortunately, too much attention has been directed to the failure of the scheme for continuation schools of the 1918
Education Act, so blurring realization of the other,
vital, successful work accomplished under other provisions.

It is to be deeply regretted that the economic crisis
of the early 1920s arrested the development of the majority of the continuation schools; as a result it has never
been possible to assess their worth as schools and their
potential contribution to educational progress.   It must
be remembered also that R.A. Butler was no more successful
in having his proposals for nursery schools and county
colleges implemented than H.A.L. Fisher.

By 1925, local education authorities were asked by the
Board of Education to submit schemes of development which
covered a period of three to five years and by so doing
to carry out the policy contained in the Fisher Act which
had placed the initiative for the development of education
upon them; had asked that authorities consult each other
and such interested parties as parents, and had also
requested them, through the scheme procedure, to look at
the needs of education in their areas as a whole.   This
action followed the easing of the economic tension in the
middle 1920s when the country was able to give fuller
attention to the recommendations of the 1918 Education Act
which rose like a phoenix from the ashes.   A significant
action towards the end of 1923 had been the withdrawal of
Circular 1190 issued in January 1921.   From now on the
Board of Education was prepared to revert to their former
practice of considering on their merits all proposals
dealing with educational development submitted by the
local education authorities (RBE, 1922-3, 1).

In conclusion, in the fifty-two sections of the 1918
Education Act, attention was paid to the grave and
increasing demands for social and educational reform which
had been made since the passing of the Balfour Act and
which had magnified during the First World War.   The far-
reaching developments in the early years of the twentieth
century - such as the changing pattern of the schools

reflecting the shifting social and economic forces and the growing interest in all influences affecting a child's life from birth to adolescence - were also encapsulated in the interlocking reforms of the Fisher Education Act. The result was that many of the weaknesses in the education system which had been apparent before the First World War were removed. A firm framework was thus provided on which future reformers could build. Because of this, the Education Act 1918 can be placed in the same category as the 1870, 1902 and 1944 Education Acts as a legislative measure of the first importance.

Education Act, 1918
(8 & 9 Geo. 5 ch. 39)
A.D. 1918

ARRANGEMENT OF SECTIONS

NATIONAL SYSTEM OF PUBLIC EDUCATION

ATTENDANCE AT SCHOOL AND EMPLOYMENT OF CHILDREN AND YOUNG PERSONS

EXTENSION OF POWERS AND DUTIES

ABOLITION OF FEES IN PUBLIC ELEMENTARY SCHOOLS

ADMINISTRATIVE PROVISIONS

Appointed days under the Education Act, 1918

Sections	Appointed Day
1 to 5	1 August 1919
6	1 November 1918
7	8 August 1918
8 (1)* and (2)*	Not yet in operation
8 (3)	2 December 1918
8 (4) and (5)	1 August 1919
8 (6), (7) and (8)	9 August 1918
9	1 February 1919
10	Not yet in operation
11 and 12	1 May 1920
13 (1) paragraphs (i) and (ii)	1 April 1920
13 (1) paragraphs (iii) and (iv)	1 April 1919
13 (2) except paragraph (iii)	1 April 1920
13 (2) paragraph (iii)	8 August 1921
14	Not yet in operation
15	8 August 1918
16 except paragraphs (c) and (d)	8 August 1918
16 paragraphs (c) and (d)	1 May 1920
17	8 August 1918
18 except so far as it imposes a duty on local education authorities	8 August 1918
18 so far as not already in operation	1 April 1920
19	8 August 1918
20	1 April 1920
21	8 August 1918
22	27 November 1918
23,24 and 25	8 August 1918
26	1 April 1919
27	8 August 1918
28	1 April 1919

Sections	Appointed Day
29 to 37	8 August 1918
38	2 December 1918
39	8 August 1918
40 except as to enquiries pending on 8 August 1918	8 August 1918
41	8 August 1918
42	1 April 1919
43	8 August 1918
44 so much of subsection (4) as refers to Small Population Grant	1 October 1918
44 (6)	1 November 1918
44 except subsection (6) and so much of subsection (4) as refers to Small Population Grant	1 April 1919
45 to 49	8 August 1918
50 except so far as it may have been brought into operation on 8 August 1918	1 May 1920
52	8 August 1918

51 was partially brought into operation from time to time
so far as it was consequential upon other sections brought
into operation.

* Under Section 52(3) the Appointed Day could not be
  earlier than the termination of the First World War.

Index of parliamentary debates on the Education Bill, 1918

Stage	Date	Volume	Columns
EDUCATION (No.1) BILL, 1917			
H.C.	1917		
		5th Series	
Introduction and First Reading	10 Aug.	97	797-854
Mr Bonar Law's Statement	19 Oct.	98	376-7
H.L.		5th Series	
Lord Curzon's Statement	22 Nov.	26	1128
H.C.		5th Series	
Mr Bonar Law's Statement as to ppd. introduction of new Bill	13 Dec.	100	1360-2
EDUCATION (No.2) BILL, 1918			
H.C.	1918		
Introduction and First Reading (under 10 Minutes rule)	14 Jan.	101	53-6

Stage	Date	Volume	Columns
EDUCATION BILL, 1918			
H.C.			
Introduction and			
First Reading	25 Feb.	103	1099
			(no debate)
Second Reading	13 Mar.	104	333-445
	18 Mar.	104	671-777
H.C.			
Committee	20 Mar.	104	1130
	3 July	107	1733-801
Report and Third	15 July	108	721-859
Reading	16 July		896-983
H.L.		5th Series	
First Reading	17 July	30	922
			(no debate)
Second Reading	23 July	30	1007-48
	24 July	30	1114-59
Committee	31 July	31	143-233*
	1 Aug.	31	250-368
Report and Third			
Reading	5 Aug.	31	495-523**
EDUCATION BILL, 1918			
H.C.	1918		
		5th Series	
Consideration of			
Lords' Amendments	6 Aug.	109	1292-304***
Royal Assent			
		5th Series	
House of Lords	8 Aug.	31	680
		5th Series	
House of Commons	8 Aug.	109	1559

*   Motion to go into Committee - Cols 143-73
**   Third Reading - Cols 517-23.
*** Motion for Consideration of Amendments - Cols 1292-4.

Suggestions for further reading

There is no substitute for gaining knowledge of the 1918
Education Act than reading the statute itself. This is
published by HMSO and should be available in any library
specializing in education. The text of the 1917 Bill can
be read in the 'Schoolmaster', 18 August 1917, and the
notes on certain clauses of the Bill, issued as a White
Paper, appear in the 'TES', 30 August 1917. The text of
the 1918 Bill was reprinted in the 'Schoolmaster', 19
January 1918, and notes issued by the Board of Education
indicating the main points of difference between the Education (No.2) Bill and the Education Bill introduced in
August were reprinted in the 'TES', 24 January 1918. The
account in Hansard of the debates in the Houses of Commons
and Lords on the Education Bills 1917 and 1918 also repays
study.

Stimulating and contradictory views can be found in the
numerous periodicals, journals and newspapers of the
period. In addition to those mentioned in the Bibliography, there are the 'Athenaeum', the 'Hibbert Journal'
the 'Nineteenth Century and After', the 'Fortnightly
Review', the 'Quarterly Review', the 'English Review'
and the 'Englishwoman'.

Of the many histories of the First World War, Sir Basil
Liddell Hart's 'History of the First World War' (latest
edition, Cassell, 1970), has long been recognized as a
standard work of reference, while Charles H. Gibbs-Smith's
'Aviation' (HMSO, 1970), adds an extra dimension to an
understanding of the war. Works by Winston Churchill provide a stimulating account of the periods preceding and
following the First World War.

H.A.L. Fisher's own 'A History of Europe' (to 1935)
(first published by Eyre & Spottiswoode in 1935) is still
read. 'The Art of the Possible, The Memoirs of Lord
Butler' (Hamish Hamilton, 1971), is not only an aid for

appreciating twentieth century politics but also a study of educational developments. Stephen Roskill's volumes, 'Hankey, Man of Secrets' (Collins, 1970), provide much new material about twentieth century political and military history.

Bibliography

WAR CABINET PAPERS (WCP)

(a) Reports of the President of the Board of Education
     to the War Cabinet

No.	Date	PRO CAB
GT 128	16 March 1917	24/7
GT 186	16 March 1917	24/7
GT 258	23 March 1917	24/8
GT 510	20 April 1917	24/11
GT 575	27 April 1917	24/11
GT 601-700	4 May 1917	24/12
GT 708	11 May 1917	24/13
GT 708	9 June 1917	24/15
GT 849	26 May 1917	24/14
GT 902	1 June 1917	24/15
GT 993	13 July 1917	24/20
GT 1066	16 June 1917	24/16
GT 1149	22 June 1917	24/17
GT 1472	20 July 1917	24/20
GT 1537	27 July 1917	24/21
GT 1761	17 August 1917	24/23
GT 2828	30 November 1917	24/34
GT 3391	18 January 1918	24/39
GT 4014	22 March 1918	24/46
GT 4581	17 May 1918	24/51

(b) Minutes of War Cabinet meetings (WCP, WC)

No.	Date	PRO CAB
WC 75	20 February 1917	23/1

WC 150	30 May 1917	23/2
WC 217(20)	17 August 1917	23/3
WC 236(2)	19 September 1917	23/4
WC 236(10)	19 September 1917	23/4
WC 274	15 November 1917	23/4
WC 298	14 December 1917	23/4

(c)   Other documents (WCP-O)

GT 757   Memorandum on the Education Bill 1917, H.A.L.
          Fisher, 16 May 1917. PRO CAB 24/13
GT 961   Employment of Children Act 1903, H.A.L. Fisher,
          4 June 1917. PRO CAB 24/15.
GT 961a   Education Bill 1917, Clause 13. 'Employment of
          Children Act 1903'. Memorandum by Sir George
          Cave, Home Office, 13 June 1917. PRO CAB 24/15.
GT 1304   Reconstruction Committee, Memorandum on the
          Education Bill 1917, June 1917. PRO CAB 24/19.
GT 1305   Reconstruction Committee, Memorandum of the Com-
          mittee on the Final Report of the Departmental
          Committee on Juvenile Education in relation to
          Employment after the War, May 1917. PRO CAB
          24/19.
GT 1601   Memorandum, 'Pensions for Teachers', 1 August
          1917, H.A.L. Fisher. PRO CAB 24/22.
GT 1604   Reconstruction Committee, Memorandum on the
          Education Bill 1917, Clause 13. 'Employment of
          Children Act, 1903'. PRO CAB 24/22.
GT 2060   Proposed formula for Higher Education Finance,
          18 September 1917, H.A.L. Fisher. PRO CAB 24/26.
GT 2459   Memorandum on the Education Bill 1917, 31 October
          1917, H.A.L. Fisher. PRO CAB 24/30.

CABINET PAPERS (CP)

CP 2346   Cabinet. Finance Committee. National Expendi-
            ture, 10 December 1920. PRO CAB 24/117.
CP 2344   Cabinet. Finance Committee. Expenditure on
            Education, 21 December 1920. PRO CAB 24/117.
27/22/5   Minutes of Cabinet meeting, 16 May 1922. PRO CAB
            23/30.
HAC 112(1)(a)   Minutes of Cabinet meeting, 13 June 1922.
            PRO CAB 23/30.

REPORTS OF THE BOARD OF EDUCATION (RBE) (1914-24)

REPORTS OF THE CHIEF MEDICAL OFFICER (1914-24)

BOARD OF EDUCATION PAPERS (BEP)

(21 May 1917) Account of meeting of L.A. Selby-Bigge with
Archbishop of Canterbury. PRO. Ed. 24/800.
(11 July 1917) Roman Catholic Schools. Minute Paper.
PRO. Ed. 24/799.
(1918) History of the Education Bill (1900). PRO. Ed.
24/2077.
(1918-32) Scheme Files. PRO. Ed. 120. Also PRO. Ed. 13
and Ed. 75.
(30 December 1919) Brighton, Education Act 1918. PRO. Ed.
120/121.
(May 1920) Kent Education Committee, The Day Continuation
School, pamphlet by E. Salter Davies, Director of
Education. PRO. Ed. 120/41.
(27 July 1920) Yorkshire W. Riding, Scheme of Education.
PRO. Ed. 120/110.
(1920) Lancashire Education Committee, Interim Scheme.
PRO. Ed. 120/49.
(21 July 1920) London County Council, Scheme of the LEA.
PRO. Ed. 120/64.
(8 December 1920) Cabinet Resolution. PRO. Ed. 24/1443.
(1920) Correspondence between the President and the
Chancellor of the Exchequer (J. Austen Chamberlain)
with regard to the application, to the Public Service
of Education, of the Cabinet Resolution of December 8th
on Expenditure. PRO. Ed. 24/1443.
(1920-2) Suggested postponement of Continuation Schools.
PRO. Ed. 24/1443.
(1920-1) Resolutions in favour of suspension of the Education Act, 1918. PRO. Ed. 24/806.
(24 January 1921) Kent Education Committee, Draft Scheme
of Education for Kent under the Education Act, 1918.
PRO. Ed. 120/41.
(1921) East Sussex Education Committee, Scheme of Education. PRO. Ed. 120/96.
(1923) By-laws raising the age of Elementary School
Attendance to 15. Letter from E.F.L. Wood to
S. Baldwin dated 6 March 1923 and reply of S. Baldwin
dated 21 March 1923. PRO Ed. 24/1537.
(1924) Memorandum by Mr W.R. Davies (Board of Education)
on day continuation schools. PRO Ed. 24/1449

MINISTRY OF EDUCATION PAPERS (MEP)

(1919-47) Further Education: Day Continuation Schools:
   Files. PRO. Ed. 75.

OFFICIAL REPORTS

(a) Consultative Committee of the Board of Education
     (1899-1944)

(1908) School Attendance of Children below the Age of
Five Years (Dyke Acland).
(1908) Question of Devolution by County Education Authorities (Dyke Acland).
(1909) Attendance, Compulsory or otherwise, at Continuation Schools (Dyke Acland).
(1926) The Education of the Adolescent (Hadow).
(1938) Secondary Education, with special reference to
Grammar Schools and Technical High Schools (Spens).

(b) Departmental Committees (Board of Education)

(1914) Local Taxation, England and Wales (Kempe).
(1917) Juvenile Education in Relation to Employment after
the War (Lewis).

(c) Interdepartmental Committees

(1909) 'Partial Exemption from School Attendance'
(Trevelyan).

(d) Secondary Schools Examination Council (established
     1917)

(1960) Secondary School Examinations other than the GCE
(Beloe).

(e) (1968) First Report of the Public Schools Commission
     (Newsom).

PRIVATE PAPERS (PP)

ASSOCIATION OF ASSISTANT MASTERS, London. Reports.

ASSOCIATION OF ASSISTANT MISTRESSES, London. Reports.
ASSOCIATION OF EDUCATION COMMITTEES, London. Reports of
Executive Committee.
ASSOCIATION OF HEADMASTERS, London. Reports.
ASSOCIATION OF HEADMISTRESSES, London. Reports.
ASSOCIATION OF TEACHERS IN TECHNICAL INSTITUTIONS, London.
Reports.
BAPTIST UNION OF GREAT BRITAIN AND IRELAND, London.
Reports of the Council.
BRITISH AND FOREIGN SCHOOL SOCIETY, London. Reports.
CATHOLIC EDUCATION COUNCIL, London. Reports.
CBI (CONFEDERATION OF BRITISH INDUSTRIES. The Federation
of British Industries became the CBI on 30 July 1965),
London. Bulletin of the FBI.
CONGREGATIONAL UNION OF ENGLAND AND WALES, London. Min-
utes of the Education Committee.
CONVOCATION OF CANTERBURY, Canterbury, Kent. The
Chronicle of Convocation, Being a Record of the Proceed-
ings of the Convocation of Canterbury.
CONVOCATION OF YORK, York. The Journal of the Convocation
of York.
COTTON SPINNERS' AND MANUFACTURERS' ASSOCIATION,
Manchester. Minutes. (The Cotton Spinners' and Manu-
facturers' Association is now called The United Kingdom
Textile Manufacturers' Association, Manchester, and the
Federation of Master Cotton Spinners' Association is now
named the British Spinners' and Doublers' Association.
The archives of the FMCS were destroyed by enemy bombing
during the Second World War.)
DURHAM EDUCATION COMMITTEE, Durham. Minutes.
ENGINEERING AND THE NATIONAL EMPLOYERS' FEDERATIONS,
London. Education Act, 1918, Memorandum as to the compul-
sory attendance of young persons at Continuation Schools,
30 November 1920. (The Engineering and the National
Employers' Federations is now known as the Engineering
Employers' Federation.)
FISHER, H.A.L. Diary. Department of Western MSS, Bodleian
Library, University of Oxford.
FRIENDS, SOCIETY OF, London. Minutes, Central Education
Committee.
LABOUR PARTY, London. Conference Reports.
LANCASHIRE EDUCATION COMMITTEE, Lancashire. Report of
Special Sub-Committee appointed to consider the Education
Bill 1917, October 1917. Education Bill 1917, Memorandum
by the Director of Education, October 1917.
LIBERAL PARTY, London. National Liberal Club, Gladstone
Library. The Government's Record 1906-13 (Seven Years of
Liberal Legislation and Liberal Administration), 1913.
The Liberal Magazine (forming a political record for the

year 1917), XXV.
LCC (LONDON COUNTY COUNCIL), London. LCC Minutes of
Proceedings.
NATIONAL COUNCIL OF THE EVANGELICAL FREE CHURCHES, London.
Reports.
NATIONAL FEDERATION OF RETAIL NEWSAGENTS, BOOKSELLERS AND
STATIONERS, London. Minutes.
NATIONAL SOCIETY, London. Minutes of the Standing
Committee.
NUT (NATIONAL UNION OF TEACHERS), London. Decisions of
Conference and Executive Classified.
PRESBYTERIAN CHURCH OF ENGLAND, London. Minutes of the
Synod.
TRADES UNION CONGRESS, London. Reports.
WESLEYAN COMMITTEE OF EDUCATION, London. Reports.

BOOKS, PAMPHLETS, JOURNALS AND NEWSPAPERS

ADAMS, J. (1917), The Teacher and his Masters, 'Contem-
porary Review', August.
AMA, organ of the Association of Assistant Masters.
ANDREWS, L. (1972) The School Meals Service, 'British
Journal of Educational Studies', February.
ARMYTAGE, W.H.G. (1964), 'Four Hundred Years of English
Education', Cambridge University Press.
ASHBY, E. and ANDERSON, M. (1974) 'Portrait of Haldane at
Work on Education', Macmillan.
ASHWORTH, W. (1960), 'An Economic History of England',
Methuen.
BAMFORD, T.W. (1967) 'The Rise of the Public Schools',
Nelson.
BARNARD, H.C. (1961) 'A History of English Education from
1760', University of London Press.
BECK, G.A. (ed.) (1950) 'The English Catholics 1850-1950',
Burns Oates.
BELL, G.K.A. (1952) 'Randall Davidson', Oxford University
Press.
BERNBAUM, G. (1967) 'Social Change and the Schools 1918-
1944', Routledge & Kegan Paul.
BIRCHENOUGH, H.C. (1925) 'History of Elementary Education',
University Tutorial Press.
'Bolton Journal and Guardian'.
'Boys' Brigade Gazette', organ of the Boys' Brigade.
'Bradford Daily Telegraph'.
'British Medical Journal', organ of the medical profes-
sion.
BROWN, C.K. FRANCIS (1942) 'The Church's Part in Education
1833-1941', National Society.

BULLOCK, A. (1960) 'The Life and Times of Ernest Bevin', Heinemann.
BURGESS, H.J. and WELSBY, P.A. (1961) 'A Short History of the National Society, 1811-1961', National Society.
'Burnley Express and Advertiser'.
'Catholic Times and Catholic Opinion', organ of the Catholic Church.
'Chief Scouts' Outlook', Headquarters Gazette, organ of the Boy Scouts.
'Christian World', organ of the Free Churches.
'Church Times', organ of the Church of England.
CCA (COUNTY COUNCILS ASSOCIATION), 'The Official Gazette of the CCA'.
CRUIKSHANK, M. (1963) 'Church and State in English Education, 1870 to the Present Day', Macmillan.
CURTIS, S.J. (1948) 'History of Education in Great Britain', University of London Press.
'Daily Mail'.
'Daily News'.
DEAN, D.W. (1970) H.A.L. Fisher, Reconstruction and the Development of the 1918 Education Act, 'British Journal of Educational Studies', October.
DICEY, A.V. (1914) 'Law and Public Opinion in England', Macmillan.
'Education': Primary, Secondary and Technical. The official educational organ of the County Councils' Association, the Association of Directors and Secretaries for Education, the Association of Technical Institutions, the Association of Teachers in Technical Institutions and the Association of Teachers of Domestic Subjects; officially recognized by numerous other educational associations.
EDUCATION REFORM COUNCIL (1917), 'Education Reform, being The Report of the Education Reform Council, published for the Teachers' Guild of Great Britain and Ireland', King.
'Engineering'.
FABIAN SOCIETY, THE (1918) 'The Teacher in Politics', Fabian Tract 187, Sidney Webb, September.
FERGUSON, R.W. and ABBOTT, A. (1935) 'Day Continuation Schools', Pitman.
FISHER, H.A.L. (1918) 'Educational Reform', Oxford University Press.
FISHER, H.A.L. (1923a) Six Years of Education in England, 'Yale Review', April.
FISHER, H.A.L. (1923b) Lines of Advance in Education, 'Contemporary Review', October.
FISHER, H.A.L. (1940) 'An Unfinished Autobiography', Oxford University Press.
'Friend', organ of the Friends' Society.

'Friends' Quarterly Examiner', organ of the Friends'
Society.
GEORGE, DAVID LLOYD (1933) 'War Memoirs of David Lloyd
George', Nicholson & Watson.
GRAVES, J. (1940) 'Policy and Progress in Secondary
Education'. Nelson.
'Highway', organ of the W.E.A.
HOARE, S.J.G. (1914) 'The Schools and Social Reform':
Report of the Unionist Social Reform Committee on Educa-
tion, Murray.
JENKINS, E.W. (1973a) The Board of Education and the
Reconstruction Committee, 1916-18, 'Journal of Educa-
tional Administration and History', University of Leeds,
January.
JENKINS, E.W. (1973b) The Thomson Committee and the Board
of Education 1916-1922, 'British Journal of Educational
Studies', University of Leeds, February.
'Jewish Chronicle', organ of the Jewish Church.
JOHNSON, P.B. (1968) 'Land Fit For Heroes, The Planning of
British Reconstruction 1916-1919', University of Chicago
Press.
'Journal of Education'.
'Journal of Education and School World'.
'Justice', organ with radical sympathies.
KEELING, F. (1914) 'Child Labour in the United Kingdom',
King.
KITCHEN, P.I. (1944) 'Birth and Growth of a Young People's
College' (Rugby), Faber.
LAWSON, J. and SILVER, H. (1973) 'A Social History of
Education in England', Methuen.
'Liverpool Daily Post and Mercury'.
'Manchester City News'.
'Manchester Guardian'.
'Methodist Recorder', organ of the Methodists.
'ME', The Report of the Ministry of Education, 1950,
Education 1900-1950 (1951), HMSO.
MOWAT, C.L. (1956) 'Britain between the Wars 1918-40',
Methuen.
'Observer'.
OGG, D. (1947) 'Herbert Fisher 1865-1940', Arnold.
PEASE, J.A. (1917) A National System of Education for
England and Wales, 'Contemporary Review', February.
'Preparatory Schools Review', organ of Incorporated
Association of Preparatory Schools.
'Presbyterian Message', organ of the Presbyterian Church.
'Preston Catholic News'.
PRITCHARD, D.G. (1963) 'Education and the Handicapped
1760-1960', Routledge & Kegan Paul.
'Record', organ of the Evangelical Church.

107 Bibliography

'Rochdale Times'.
'Schoolmaster', organ of the National Union of Teachers.
'Secondary Education', organ of the Private Schools
Association.
SELBY-BIGGE, Sir L.A. (1934) 'The Board of Education',
Putnam.
SHERINGTON, G.E. (1974) R.B. Haldane, The Reconstruction
Committee and the Board of Education, 1916-18, 'Journal of
Educational Administration and History', University of
Leeds, July.
SIMON, B. (1965) 'Education and the Labour Movement 1870-
1920', Lawrence & Wishart.
SIMON, B. (1974) 'The Politics of Educational Reform',
Lawrence & Wishart.
STEWART, W.A.C. (1972) 'Progressives and Radicals in
English Education 1750-1970', Macmillan.
'Tablet', organ of the Roman Catholic Church.
'Tablet Educational Supplement', organ of the Roman
Catholic Curch.
TAWNEY, R.H. (1964) 'The Radical Tradition', Allen &
Unwin.
TAYLOR, A.J.P. (1965) 'English History 1914-1945',Oxford.
THOMS, D.W. (1974) The Education Act of 1918 and the
Development of Central Government Control of Education,
'Journal of Educational Administration and History', Uni-
versity of Leeds, July.
THOMS, D.W. (1975) The Emergence and Failure of the Day
Continuation School Experiment, 'History of Education'
(Journal of the History of Education Society), Spring.
THOMSON, D. (1965) 'England in the Twentieth Century
(1914-63)', Penguin (Pelican History of England).
'Times, The'
'TES', 'The Times Educational Supplement' (weekly).
TROPP, A. (1957) 'The School Teachers', Heinemann.
VAIZEY, J. and SHEEHAN, J. (1968) 'Resources for Educa-
tion', Allen & Unwin.
WATERFALL, E.A. (1923) 'The Day Continuation School in
England', Allen & Unwin.
WEBB, S. (1918) 'The Teacher in Politics', Fabian Tract
No.187.
'Westminster Gazette'.
WHITEHOUSE, J.H. (1913) 'A National System of Education',
Cambridge University Press.
WORKERS' EDUCATION ASSOCIATION (1918) 'The Choice of the
Nation. Some Amendments to the Education Bill', April.
'Yorkshire Post'.